Essays on Political Economy

Frédéric Bastiat

CAPITAL AND INTEREST.

My object in this treatise is to examine into the real nature of the Interest of Capital, for the purpose of proving that it is lawful, and explaining why it should be perpetual. This may appear singular, and yet, I confess, I am more afraid of being too plain than too obscure. I am afraid I may weary the reader by a series of mere truisms. But it is no easy matter to avoid this danger, when the facts with which we have to deal are known to every one by personal, familiar, and daily experience.

But, then, you will say, "What is the use of this treatise? Why explain what everybody knows?"

But, although this problem appears at first sight so very simple, there is more in it than you might suppose. I shall endeavour to prove this by an example. Mondor lends an instrument of labour to-day, which will be entirely destroyed in a week, yet the capital will not produce the less interest to Mondor or his heirs, through all eternity. Reader, can you honestly say that you understand the reason of this?

It would be a waste of time to seek any satisfactory explanation from the writings of economists. They have not thrown much light upon the reasons of the existence of interest. For this they are not to be blamed; for at the time they wrote, its lawfulness was not called in question. Now, however, times are altered; the case is different. Men, who consider themselves to be in advance of their age, have organised an active crusade against capital and interest; it is the productiveness of capital which they are attacking; not certain abuses in the administration of it, but the principle itself.

A journal has been established to serve as a vehicle for this crusade. It is conducted by M. Proudhon, and has, it is said, an immense circulation. The first number of this periodical contains the electoral manifesto of the people. Here we read, "The productiveness of capital, which is condemned by Christianity under the name of usury, is the true cause of misery, the true principle of destitution, the eternal obstacle to the establishment of the Republic."

Another journal, La Ruche Populaire, after having said some excellent things on labour, adds, "But, above all, labour ought to be free; that is, it ought to be organised in such a manner, that *money-lenders and patrons, or masters, should not be paid for this liberty of labour, this right of labour,* which is raised to so high a price by the traffickers of men." The only thought that I notice here, is that expressed by the words in italics, which imply a denial of the right to interest. The remainder of the article explains it.

It is thus that the democratic Socialist, Thoré expresses himself:--

"The revolution will always have to be recommenced, so long as we occupy ourselves with consequences only, without having the logic or the courage to attack the principle itself. This principle is capital, false property, interest, and usury, which by the old régime, is made to weigh upon labour.

"Ever since the aristocrats invented the incredible fiction, that capital possesses the power of reproducing itself, the workers have been at the mercy of the idle.

"At the end of a year, will you find an additional crown in a bag of one hundred shillings? At the end of fourteen years, will your shillings have doubled in your bag?

"Will a work of industry or of skill produce another, at the end of fourteen years?

"Let us begin, then, by demolishing this fatal fiction."

I have quoted the above, merely for the sake of establishing the fact, that many persons consider the productiveness of capital a false, a fatal, and an iniquitous principle. But quotations are superfluous; it is well known that the people attribute their sufferings to what they call the trafficking in man by man. In fact, the phrase, tyranny of capital, has become proverbial.

I believe there is not a man in the world, who is aware of the whole importance of this question:--

"Is the interest of capital natural, just, and lawful, and as useful to the payer as to the receiver?"

You answer, No; I answer, Yes. Then we differ entirely; but it is of the utmost importance to discover which of us is in the right, otherwise we shall incur the danger of making a false solution of the question, a matter of opinion. If the error is on my side, however, the evil would not be so great. It must be inferred that I know nothing about the true interests of the masses, or the march of human progress; and that all my arguments are but as so many grains of sand, by which the car of the revolution will certainly not be arrested.

But if, on the contrary, MM. Proudhon and Thoré are deceiving themselves, it follows that they are leading the people astray--that they are showing them the evil where it does not exist; and thus giving a false direction to their ideas, to their antipathies, to their dislikes, and to their attacks. It follows that the misguided people are rushing into a horrible and absurd struggle, in which victory would be more fatal than defeat; since, according to this supposition, the result would be the realisation of universal evils, the destruction of every means of emancipation, the consummation of its own misery.

This is just what M. Proudhon has acknowledged, with perfect good faith. "The foundation stone," he told me, "of my system is thegratuitousness of credit. If I am mistaken in this, Socialism is a vain dream." I add, it is a dream, in which the people are tearing themselves to pieces. Will it, therefore, be a cause for surprise, if, when they awake, they find themselves mangled and bleeding? Such a danger as this is enough to justify me fully, if, in the course of the discussion, I allow myself to be led into some trivialities and some prolixity.

I address this treatise to the workmen of Paris, more especially to those who have enrolled themselves under the banner of Socialist democracy. I proceed to consider these two questions:--

1st. Is it consistent with the nature of things, and with justice, that capital should produce interest?

2nd. Is it consistent with the nature of things, and with justice, that the interest of capital should be perpetual?

The working men of Paris will certainly acknowledge that a more important subject could not be discussed.

Since the world began, it has been allowed, at least in part, that capital ought to produce interest. But latterly it has been affirmed, that herein lies the very social error which is the cause of pauperism and inequality. It is, therefore, very essential to know now on what ground we stand.

For if levying interest from capital is a sin, the workers have a right to revolt against social order, as it exists. It is in vain to tell them that they ought to have recourse to legal and pacific means: it would be a hypocritical recommendation. When on the one side there is a strong man, poor, and a victim of robbery--on the other, a weak man, but rich, and a robber--it is singular enough that we should say to the former, with a hope of persuading him, "Wait till your oppressor voluntarily renounces oppression, or till it shall cease of itself." This cannot be; and those who tell us that capital is by nature unproductive, ought to know that they are provoking a terrible and immediate struggle.

If, on the contrary, the interest of capital is natural, lawful, consistent with the general good, as favourable to the borrower as to the lender, the economists who deny it, the tribunes who traffic in this pretended social wound, are leading the workmen into a senseless and unjust struggle, which can have no other issue than the misfortune of all. In fact, they are arming labour against capital. So much the better, if these two powers are really antagonistic; and may the struggle soon be ended! But, if they are in harmony, the struggle is the greatest evil which can be inflicted on society. You see, then, workmen, that there is not a more important question than this:--"Is the interest of capital lawful or not?" In the former case, you must immediately renounce the struggle to which you are being urged; in the second, you must carry it on bravely, and to the end.

Productiveness of capital--perpetuity of interest. These are difficult questions. I must endeavour to make myself clear. And for that purpose I shall have recourse to example rather than to demonstration; or rather, I shall place the demonstration in the example. I begin by acknowledging that, at first sight, it may appear strange that capital should pretend to a remuneration, and above all, to a perpetual remuneration. You will say, "Here are two men. One of them works from morning till night, from one year's end to another; and if he consumes all which he has gained, even by superior energy, he remains poor. When Christmas comes he is no forwarder than he was at the beginning of the year, and has no other prospect but to begin again. The other man does nothing, either with his hands or his head; or at least, if he makes use of them at all, it is only for his own pleasure; it is allowable for him to do nothing, for he has an income. He does not work, yet he lives well; he has everything in abundance; delicate dishes, sumptuous furniture, elegant equipages; nay, he even consumes, daily, things which the workers have been obliged to produce by the sweat of their brow, for these things do not make themselves; and, as far as he is concerned, he has had no hand in their production. It is the workmen who have caused this corn to grow, polished this furniture, woven these carpets; it is our wives and daughters who have spun, cut out, sewed, and embroidered these stuffs. We work, then, for him and for ourselves; for him first, and then for ourselves, if there is anything left. But here is something more striking still. If the former of these two men, the worker, consumes within the year any profit which may have been left him in that year, he is always at the point from which he started, and his destiny condemns him to move incessantly in a perpetual circle, and a monotony of exertion. Labour, then, is rewarded only once. But if the other, the 'gentleman,' consumes his yearly income in the year, he has, the year after, in those which follow, and through all eternity, an income always equal, inexhaustible, perpetual. Capital, then, is remunerated, not only once or twice, but an indefinite number of times! So that, at the end of a hundred years, a family which has placed 20,000 francs,[1] at five per cent., will have had 100,000 francs; and this will not prevent it from having 100,000 more, in the following century. In other words, for 20,000 francs, which represent its labour, it will have levied, in two centuries, a tenfold value on the labour of others. In this social arrangement, is there not a monstrous evil to be reformed? And this is not all. If it should please this family to curtail its enjoyments a little--to spend, for example, only 900 francs, instead of 1,000--it may, without any labour, without any other trouble beyond that of investing 100 francs a year, increase its capital and its income in such rapid progression, that it will soon be in a position to consume as much as a hundred families of industrious workmen. Does not all this go to prove that society itself has in its bosom a hideous cancer, which ought to be eradicated at the risk of some temporary suffering?"

These are, it appears to me, the sad and irritating reflections which must be excited in your minds by the active and superficial crusade which is being carried on against capital and interest. On the other hand, there are moments in which, I am convinced, doubts are awakened in your minds, and scruples in your conscience. You say to yourselves sometimes, "But to assert that capital ought not to produce interest, is to say that he who has created instruments of labour, or materials, or provisions of any kind, ought to yield them up without compensation. Is that just? And then, if it is so, who would lend these instruments, these materials, these provisions? who would take care of them? who even would create them? Every one would consume his proportion, and the human race would never advance a step. Capital would be no longer formed, since there would be no interest in forming it. It would become exceedingly scarce. A singular step towards gratuitous loans! A singular means of improving the condition of borrowers, to make it impossible for them to borrow at any price! What would become of labour itself? for there will be no money advanced, and not one single kind of labour can be mentioned, not even the chase, which can be pursued without money in hand. And, as for ourselves, what would become of us? What! we are not to be allowed to borrow, in order to work in the prime of life, nor to lend, that we may enjoy repose in its decline? The law will rob us of the prospect of laying by a little property, because it will prevent us from gaining any advantage from it. It will deprive us of all stimulus to save at the present time, and of all hope of repose for the future. It is useless to exhaust ourselves with fatigue: we must abandon the idea of leaving our sons and daughters a little property, since modern science renders it useless, for we should become traffickers in men if we were to lend it on interest. Alas! the world which these persons would open before us, as an imaginary good, is still more dreary and desolate than that which they condemn, for hope, at any rate, is not banished from the latter." Thus, in all respects, and in every point of view, the question is a serious one. Let us hasten to arrive at a solution.

Our civil code has a chapter entitled, "On the manner of transmitting property." I do not think it gives a very complete nomenclature on this point. When a man by his labour has made some useful thing--in other words, when he has created a value--it can only pass into the hands of another by one of the following modes--as a gift, by the right of inheritance, by exchange, loan, or theft. One word upon each of these, except the last, although it plays a greater part in the world than we may think. A gift needs no definition. It is essentially voluntary and spontaneous. It depends exclusively upon the giver, and the receiver cannot be said to have any right to it. Without a doubt, morality and religion make it a duty for men, especially the rich, to deprive themselves voluntarily of that which they possess, in favour of their less fortunate brethren. But this is an entirely moral obligation. If it were to be asserted on principle, admitted in practice, or sanctioned by law, that every man has a right to the property of another, the gift would have no merit--charity and gratitude would be no longer virtues. Besides, such a doctrine would suddenly and universally arrest labour and production, as severe cold congeals water and suspends animation; for who would work if there was no longer to be any connection between labour and the satisfying of our wants? Political economy has not treated of gifts. It has hence been concluded that it disowns them, and that it is therefore a science devoid of heart. This is a ridiculous accusation. That science which treats of the laws resulting from the reciprocity of services, had no business to inquire into the consequences of generosity with respect to him who receives, nor into its effects, perhaps still more precious, on him who gives: such considerations belong evidently to the science of morals. We must allow the sciences to have limits; above all, we must not accuse them of denying or undervaluing what they look upon as foreign to their department.

The right of inheritance, against which so much has been objected of late, is one of the forms of gift, and assuredly the most natural of all. That which a man has produced, he may consume, exchange, or give. What can be more natural than that he should give it to his children? It is this power, more than any other, which inspires him with courage to labour and to save. Do you know why the principle of right of inheritance is thus called in question? Because it is imagined that the property thus transmitted is plundered from the masses. This is a fatal error. Political economy demonstrates, in the most peremptory manner, that all value produced is a creation which does no harm to any person whatever. For that reason it may be consumed, and, still more, transmitted, without hurting any one; but I shall not pursue these reflections, which do not belong to the subject.

Exchange is the principal department of political economy, because it is by far the most frequent method of transmitting property, according to the free and voluntary agreements of the laws and effects of which this science treats.

Properly speaking, exchange is the reciprocity of services. The parties say between themselves, "Give me this, and I will give you that;" or, "Do this for me, and I will do that for you." It is well to remark (for this will throw a new light on the notion of value) that the second form is always implied in the first. When it is said, "Do this for me, and I will do that for you," an exchange of service for service is proposed. Again, when it is said, "Give me this, and I will give you that," it is the same as saying, "I yield to you what I have done, yield to me what you have done." The labour is past, instead of present; but the exchange is not the less governed by the comparative valuation of the two services: so that it is quite correct to say that the principle of value is in the services rendered and received on account of the productions exchanged, rather than in the productions themselves.

In reality, services are scarcely ever exchanged directly. There is a medium, which is termed money. Paul has completed a coat, for which he wishes to receive a little bread, a little wine, a little oil, a visit from a doctor, a ticket for the play, &c. The exchange cannot be effected in kind, so what does Paul do? He first exchanges his coat for some money, which is called sale; then he exchanges this money again for the things which he wants, which is called purchase; and now, only, has the reciprocity of services completed its circuit; now, only, the labour and the compensation are balanced in the same individual,--"I have done this for society, it has done that for me." In a word, it is only now that the exchange is actually accomplished. Thus, nothing can be more correct than this observation of J. B. Say:--"Since the introduction of money, every exchange is resolved into two elements, sale and purchase. It is the reunion of these two elements which renders the exchange complete."

We must remark, also, that the constant appearance of money in every exchange has overturned and misled all our ideas: men have ended in thinking that money was true riches, and that to multiply it was to multiply services and products. Hence the prohibitory system; hence paper money; hence the celebrated aphorism, "What one gains the other loses;" and all the errors which have ruined the earth, and embrued it with blood.2 After much research it has been found, that in order to make the two services exchanged of equivalent value, and in order to render the exchange equitable, the best means was to allow it to be free. However plausible, at first sight, the intervention of the State might be, it was soon perceived that it is always oppressive to one or other of the contracting parties. When we look into these subjects, we are always compelled to reason upon this maxim, that equal valueresults from liberty. We have, in fact, no other means of knowing whether, at a given moment, two services are of the same value, but that of examining whether they can be readily and freely exchanged. Allow the State, which is the same thing as force, to interfere on one side or the other, and from that moment all the means of appreciation will be complicated and entangled, instead of becoming clear. It ought to be the part of the State to prevent, and, above all, to repress artifice and fraud; that is, to secure liberty, and not to violate it. I have enlarged a little upon exchange, although loan is my principal object: my excuse is, that I conceive that there is in a loan an actual exchange, an actual service rendered by the lender, and which makes the borrower liable to an equivalent service,--two services, whose comparative value can only be appreciated, like that of all possible services, by freedom. Now, if it is so, the perfect lawfulness of what is called house-rent, farm-rent, interest, will be explained and justified. Let us consider the case of loan.

Suppose two men exchange two services or two objects, whose equal value is beyond all dispute. Suppose, for example, Peter says to Paul, "Give me ten sixpences, I will give you a five-shilling piece." We cannot imagine an equal value more unquestionable. When the bargain is made, neither party has any claim upon the other. The exchanged services are equal. Thus it follows, that if one of the parties wishes to introduce into the bargain an additional clause, advantageous to himself, but unfavourable to the other party, he must agree to a second clause, which shall re-establish the equilibrium, and the law of justice. It would be absurd to deny the justice of a second clause of compensation. This granted, we will suppose that Peter, after having said to Paul, "Give me ten sixpences, I will give you a crown," adds, "You shall give me the ten sixpences now, and I will give you the crown-piece in a year;" it is very evident that this new proposition alters the claims and advantages of the bargain; that it alters the proportion of the two services. Does it not appear plainly enough, in fact, that Peter asks of Paul a new and an additional service; one of a different kind? Is it not as if he had said, "Render me the service of allowing me to use for my profit, for a year, five shillings which belong to you, and which you might have used for yourself?" And what good reason have you to maintain that Paul is bound to render this especial service gratuitously; that he has no right to demand anything more in consequence of this requisition; that the State ought to interfere to force him to submit? Is it not incomprehensible that the economist, who preaches such a doctrine to the people, can reconcile it with his principle of the reciprocity of services? Here I have introduced cash; I have been led to do so by a desire to place, side by side, two objects of exchange, of a perfect and indisputable equality of value. I was anxious to be prepared for objections; but, on the other hand, my demonstration would have been more striking still, if I had illustrated my principle by an agreement for exchanging the services or the productions themselves.

Suppose, for example, a house and a vessel of a value so perfectly equal that their proprietors are disposed to exchange them even-handed, without excess or abatement. In fact let the bargain be settled by a lawyer. At the moment of each taking possession, the shipowner says to the citizen, "Very well; the transaction is completed, and nothing can prove its perfect equity better than our free and voluntary consent. Our conditions thus fixed, I shall propose to you a little practical modification. You shall let me have your house to-day, but I shall not put you in possession of my ship for a year; and the reason I make this demand of you is, that, during this year of delay, I wish to use the vessel." That we may not be embarrassed by considerations relative to the deterioration of the thing lent, I will suppose the shipowner to add, "I will engage, at the end of the year, to hand over to you the vessel in the state in which it is to-day." I ask of every candid man, I ask of M. Proudhon himself, if the citizen has not a right to answer, "The new clause which you propose entirely alters the proportion or the equal value of the exchanged services. By it, I shall be deprived, for the space of a year, both at once of my house and of your vessel. By it, you will make use of both. If, in the absence of this clause, the bargain was just, for the same reason the clause is injurious to me. It stipulates for a loss to me, and a gain to you. You are requiring of me a new service; I have a right to refuse, or to require of you, as a compensation, an equivalent service." If the parties are agreed upon this compensation, the principle of which is incontestable, we can easily distinguish two transactions in one, two exchanges of service in one. First, there is the exchange of the house for the vessel; after this, there is the delay granted by one of the parties, and the compensation correspondent to this delay yielded by the other. These two new services take the generic and abstract names of credit and interest. But names do not change the nature of things; and I defy any one to dare to maintain that there exists here, when all is done, a service for a service, or a reciprocity of services. To say that one of these services does not challenge the other, to say that the first ought to be rendered gratuitously, without injustice, is to say that injustice consists in the reciprocity of services,--that justice consists in one of the parties giving and not receiving, which is a contradiction in terms.

To give an idea of interest and its mechanism, allow me to make use of two or three anecdotes. But, first, I must say a few words upon capital.

There are some persons who imagine that capital is money, and this is precisely the reason why they deny its productiveness; for, as M. Thoré says, crowns are not endowed with the power of reproducing themselves. But it is not true that capital and money are the same thing. Before the discovery of the precious metals, there were capitalists in the world; and I venture to say that at that time, as now, everybody was a capitalist, to a certain extent.

What is capital, then? It is composed of three things:--

1st. Of the materials upon which men operate, when these materials have already a value communicated by some human effort, which has bestowed upon them the principle of remuneration--wool, flax, leather, silk, wood, &c.

2nd. Instruments which are used for working--tools, machines, ships, carriages, &c.

3rd. Provisions which are consumed during labour--victuals, stuffs, houses, &c.

Without these things the labour of man would be unproductive and almost void; yet these very things have required much work, especially at first. This is the reason that so much value has been attached to the possession of them, and also that it is perfectly lawful to exchange and to sell them, to make a profit of them if used, to gain remuneration from them if lent.

Now for my anecdotes.

THE SACK OF CORN.

Mathurin, in other respects as poor as Job, and obliged to earn his bread by day-labour, became nevertheless, by some inheritance, the owner of a fine piece of uncultivated land. He was exceedingly anxious to cultivate it. "Alas!" said he, "to make ditches, to raise fences, to break the soil, to clear away the brambles and stones, to plough it, to sow it, might bring me a living in a year or two; but certainly not to-day, or to-morrow. It is impossible to set about farming it, without previously saving some provisions for my subsistence until the harvest; and I know, by experience, that preparatory labour is indispensable, in order to render present labour productive." The good Mathurin was not content with making these reflections. He resolved to work by the day, and to save something from his wages to buy a spade and a sack of corn; without which things, he must give up his fine agricultural projects. He acted so well, was so active and steady, that he soon saw himself in possession of the wished-for sack of corn. "I shall take it to the mill," said he, "and then I shall have enough to live upon till my field is covered with a rich harvest." Just as he was starting, Jerome came to borrow his treasure of him. "If you will lend me this sack of corn," said Jerome, "you will do me a great service; for I have some very lucrative work in view, which I cannot possibly undertake, for want of provisions to live upon until it is finished." "I was in the same case," answered Mathurin, "and if I have now secured bread for several months, it is at the expense of my arms and my stomach. Upon what principle of justice can it be devoted to the realisation of your enterprise instead of mine?"

You may well believe that the bargain was a long one. However, it was finished at length, and on these conditions:--

First--Jerome promised to give back, at the end of the year, a sack of corn of the same quality, and of the same weight, without missing a single grain. "This first clause is perfectly just," said he, "for without it Mathurin would give, and not lend."

Secondly--He engaged to deliver five litres on every hectolitre. "This clause is no less just than the other," thought he; "for without it Mathurin would do me a service without compensation; he would inflict upon himself a privation--he would renounce his cherished enterprise--he would enable me to accomplish mine--he would cause me to enjoy for a year the fruits of his savings, and all this gratuitously. Since he delays the cultivation of his land, since he enables me to realise a lucrative labour, it is quite natural that I should let him partake, in a certain proportion, of the profits which I shall gain by the sacrifice he makes of his own."

On his side, Mathurin, who was something of a scholar, made this calculation:--"Since, by virtue of the first clause, the sack of corn will return to me at the end of a year," he said to himself, "I shall be able to lend it again; it will return to me at the end of the second year; I may lend it again, and so on, to all eternity. However, I cannot deny that it will have been eaten long ago. It is singular that I should be perpetually the owner of a sack of corn, although the one I have lent has been consumed for ever. But this is explained thus:--It will be consumed in the service of Jerome. It will put it into the power of Jerome to produce a superior value; and, consequently, Jerome will be able to restore me a sack of corn, or the value of it, without having suffered the slightest injury: but quite the contrary. And as regards myself, this value ought to be my property, as long as I do not consume it myself. If I had used it to clear my land, I should have received it again in the form of a fine harvest. Instead of that, I lend it, and shall recover it in the form of repayment.

"From the second clause, I gain another piece of information. At the end of the year I shall be in possession of five litres of corn over the one hundred that I have just lent. If, then, I were to continue to work by the day, and to save part of my wages, as I have been doing, in the course of time I should be able to lend two sacks of corn; then three; then four; and when I should have gained a sufficient number to enable me to live on these additions of five litres over and above each, I shall be at liberty to take a little repose in my old age. But how is this? In this case, shall I not be living at the expense of others? No, certainly, for it has been proved that in lending I perform a service; I complete the labour of my borrowers, and only deduct a trifling part of the excess of production, due to my lendings and savings. It is a marvellous thing that a man may thus realise a leisure which injures no one, and for which he cannot be envied without injustice."

THE HOUSE.

Mondor had a house. In building it, he had extorted nothing from any one whatever. He owed it to his own personal labour, or, which is the same thing, to labour justly rewarded. His first care was to make a bargain with an architect, in virtue of which, by means of a hundred crowns a year, the latter engaged to keep the house in constant good repair. Mondor was already congratulating himself on the happy days which he hoped to spend in this retreat, declared sacred by our Constitution. But Valerius wished to make it his residence.

"How can you think of such a thing?" said Mondor to Valerius. "It is I who have built it; it has cost me ten years of painful labour, and now you would enjoy it!" They agreed to refer the matter to judges. They chose no profound economists,--there were none such in the country. But they found some just and sensible men; it all comes to the same thing; political economy, justice, good sense, are all the same thing. Now here is the decision made by the judges:--If Valerius wishes to occupy Mondor's house for a year, he is bound to submit to three conditions. The first is to quit at the end of the year, and to restore the house in good repair, saving the inevitable decay resulting from mere duration. The second, to refund to Mondor the 300 francs which the latter pays annually to the architect to repair the injuries of time; for these injuries taking place whilst the house is in the service of Valerius, it is perfectly just that he should bear the consequences. The third, that he should render to Mondor a service equivalent to that which he receives. As to this equivalence of services, it must be freely discussed between Mondor and Valerius.

THE PLANE.

A very long time ago there lived, in a poor village, a joiner, who was a philosopher, as all my heroes are in their way. James worked from morning till night with his two strong arms, but his brain was not idle for all that. He was fond of reviewing his actions, their causes, and their effects. He sometimes said to himself, "With my hatchet, my saw, and my hammer, I can make only coarse furniture, and can only get the pay for such. If I only had a plane, I should please my customers more, and they would pay me more. It is quite just; I can only expect services proportioned to those which I render myself. Yes! I am resolved, I will make myself a plane."

However, just as he was setting to work, James reflected further:--"I work for my customers 300 days in the year. If I give ten to making my plane, supposing it lasts me a year, only 290 days will remain for me to make my furniture. Now, in order that I be not the loser in this matter, I must gain henceforth, with the help of the plane, as much in 290 days, as I now do in 300. I must even gain more; for unless I do so, it would not be worth my while to venture upon any innovations." James began to calculate. He satisfied himself that he should sell his finished furniture at a price which would amply compensate for the ten days devoted to the plane; and when no doubt remained on this point, he set to work. I beg the reader to remark, that the power which exists in the tool to increase the productiveness of labour, is the basis of the solution which follows.

At the end of ten days, James had in his possession an admirable plane, which he valued all the more for having made it himself. He danced for joy,--for, like the girl with her basket of eggs, he reckoned all the profits which he expected to derive from the ingenious instrument; but, more fortunate than she, he was not reduced to the necessity of saying good-bye to calf, cow, pig, and eggs, together. He was building his fine castles in the air, when he was interrupted by his acquaintance William, a joiner in the neighbouring village. William having admired the plane, was struck with the advantages which might be gained from it. He said to James:--

W. You must do me a service.

J. What service?

W. Lend me the plane for a year.

As might be expected, James at this proposal did not fail to cry out, "How can you think of such a thing, William? Well, if I do you this service, what will you do for me in return?"

W. Nothing. Don't you know that a loan ought to be gratuitous? Don't you know that capital is naturally unproductive? Don't you know fraternity has been proclaimed. If you only do me a service for the sake of receiving one from me in return, what merit would you have?

J. William, my friend, fraternity does not mean that all the sacrifices are to be on one side; if so, I do not see why they should not be on yours. Whether a loan should be gratuitous I don't know; but I do know that if I were to lend you my plane for a year it would be giving it you. To tell you the truth, that was not what I made it for.

W. Well, we will say nothing about the modern maxims discovered by the Socialist gentlemen. I ask you to do me a service; what service do you ask me in return?

J. First, then, in a year, the plane will be done for, it will be good for nothing. It is only just, that you should let me have another exactly like it; or that you should give me money enough to get it repaired; or that you should supply me the ten days which I must devote to replacing it.

W. This is perfectly just. I submit to these conditions. I engage to return it, or to let you have one like it, or the value of the same. I think you must be satisfied with this, and can require nothing further.

J. I think otherwise. I made the plane for myself, and not for you. I expected to gain some advantage from it, by my work being better finished and better paid, by an improvement in my condition. What reason is there that I should make the plane, and you should gain the profit? I might as well ask you to give me your saw and hatchet! What a confusion! Is it not natural that each should keep what he has made with his own hands, as well as his hands themselves? To use without recompense the hands of another, I call slavery; to use without recompense the plane of another, can this be called fraternity?

W. But, then, I have agreed to return it to you at the end of a year, as well polished and as sharp as it is now.

J. We have nothing to do with next year; we are speaking of this year. I have made the plane for the sake of improving my work and condition; if you merely return it to me in a year, it is you who will gain the profit of it during the whole of that time. I am not bound to do you such a service without receiving anything from you in return: therefore, if you wish for my plane, independently of the entire restoration already bargained for, you must do me a service which we will now discuss; you must grant me remuneration.

And this was done thus:--William granted a remuneration calculated in such a way that, at the end of the year, James received his plane quite new, and in addition, a compensation, consisting of a new plank, for the advantages of which he had deprived himself, and which he had yielded to his friend.

It was impossible for any one acquainted with the transaction to discover the slightest trace in it of oppression or injustice.

The singular part of it is, that, at the end of the year, the plane came into James's possession, and he lent it again; recovered it, and lent it a third and fourth time. It has passed into the hands of his son, who still lends it. Poor plane! how many times has it changed, sometimes its blade, sometimes its handle. It is no longer the same plane, but it has always the same value, at least for James's posterity. Workmen! let us examine into these little stories.

I maintain, first of all, that the sack of corn and the plane are here the type, the model, a faithful representation, the symbol of all capital; as the five litres of corn and the plank are the type, the model, the representation, the symbol of all interest. This granted, the following are, it seems to me, a series of consequences, the justice of which it is impossible to dispute.

1st. If the yielding of a plank by the borrower to the lender is a natural, equitable, lawful remuneration, the just price of a real service, we may conclude that, as a general rule, it is in the nature of capital to produce interest. When this capital, as in the foregoing examples, takes the form of an instrument of labour, it is clear enough that it ought to bring an advantage to its possessor, to him who has devoted to it his time, his brains, and his strength. Otherwise, why should he have made it? No necessity of life can be immediately satisfied with instruments of labour; no one eats planes or drinks saws, except, indeed, he be a conjuror. If a man determines to spend his time in the production of such things, he must have been led to it by the consideration of the power which these instruments add to his power; of the time which they save him; of the perfection and rapidity which they give to his labour; in a word, of the advantages which they procure for him. Now, these advantages, which have been prepared by labour, by the sacrifice of time which might have been used in a more immediate manner, are we bound, as soon as they are ready to be enjoyed, to confer them gratuitously upon another? Would it be an advance in social order, if the law decided thus, and citizens should pay officials for causing such a law to be executed by force? I venture to say, that there is not one amongst you who would support it. It would be to legalize, to organize, to systematize injustice itself, for it would be proclaiming that there are men born to render, and others born to receive, gratuitous services. Granted, then, that interest is just, natural, and lawful.

2nd. A second consequence, not less remarkable than the former, and, if possible, still more conclusive, to which I call your attention, is this:-- Interest is not injurious to the borrower. I mean to say, the obligation in which the borrower finds himself, to pay a remuneration for the use of capital, cannot do any harm to his condition. Observe, in fact, that James and William are perfectly free, as regards the transaction to which the plane gave occasion. The transaction cannot be accomplished without the consent of the one as well as of the other. The worst which can happen is, that James may be too exacting; and in this case, William, refusing the loan, remains as he was before. By the fact of his agreeing to borrow, he proves that he considers it an advantage to himself; he proves, that after every calculation, including the remuneration, whatever it may be, required of him, he still finds it more profitable to borrow than not to borrow. He only determines to do so because he has compared the inconveniences with the advantages. He has calculated that the day on which he returns the plane, accompanied by the remuneration agreed upon, he will have effected more work, with the same labour, thanks to this tool. A profit will remain to him, otherwise he would not have borrowed. The two services of which we are speaking are exchanged according to the law which governs all exchanges, the law of supply and demand. The claims of James have a natural and impassable limit. This is the point in which the remuneration demanded by him would absorb all the advantage which William might find in making use of a plane. In this case, the borrowing would not take place. William would be bound either to make a plane for himself, or to do without one, which would leave him in his original condition. He borrows, because he gains by borrowing. I know very well what will be told me. You will say, William may be deceived, or, perhaps, he may be governed by necessity, and be obliged to submit to a harsh law.

It may be so. As to errors in calculation, they belong to the infirmity of our nature, and to argue from this against the transaction in question, is objecting the possibility of loss in all imaginable transactions, in every human act. Error is an accidental fact, which is incessantly remedied by experience. In short, everybody must guard against it. As far as those hard necessities are concerned, which force persons to burdensome borrowings, it is clear that these necessities exist previously to the borrowing. If William is in a situation in which he cannot possibly do without a plane, and must borrow one at any price, does this situation result from James having taken the trouble to make the tool? Does it not exist independently of this circumstance? However harsh, however severe James may be, he will never render the supposed condition of William worse than it is. Morally, it is true, the lender will be to blame; but, in an economical point of view, the loan itself can never be considered responsible for previous necessities, which it has not created, and which it relieves to a certain extent.

But this proves something to which I shall return. The evident interests of William, representing here the borrowers, there are many Jameses and planes, in other words, lenders and capitals. It is very evident, that if

William can say to James,--"Your demands are exorbitant; there is no lack of planes in the world;" he will be in a better situation than if James's plane was the only one to be borrowed. Assuredly, there is no maxim more true than this--service for service. But left us not forget that no service has a fixed and absolute value, compared with others. The contracting parties are free. Each carries his requisitions to the farthest possible point, and the most favourable circumstance for these requisitions is the absence of rivalship. Hence it follows, that if there is a class of men more interested than any other in the formation, multiplication, and abundance of capitals, it is mainly that of the borrowers. Now, since capitals can only be formed and increased by the stimulus and the prospect of remuneration, let this class understand the injury they are inflicting on themselves when they deny the lawfulness of interest, when they proclaim that credit should be gratuitous, when they declaim against the pretended tyranny of capital, when they discourage saving, thus forcing capitals to become scarce, and consequently interests to rise.

3rd. The anecdote I have just related enables you to explain this apparently singular phenomenon, which is termed the duration or perpetuity of interest. Since, in lending his plane, James has been able, very lawfully, to make it a condition that it should be returned to him, at the end of a year, in the same state in which it was when he lent it, is it not evident that he may, at the expiration of the term, lend it again on the same conditions? If he resolves upon the latter plan, the plane will return to him at the end of every year, and that without end. James will then be in a condition to lend it without end; that is, he may derive from it a perpetual interest. It will be said, that the plane will be worn out. That is true; but it will be worn out by the hand and for the profit of the borrower. The latter has taken into account this gradual wear, and taken upon himself, as he ought, the consequences. He has reckoned that he shall derive from this tool an advantage, which will allow him to restore it in its original condition, after having realised a profit from it. As long as James does not use this capital himself, or for his own advantage--as long as he renounces the advantages which allow it to be restored to its original condition--he will have an incontestable right to have it restored, and that independently of interest.

Observe, besides, that if, as I believe I have shown, James, far from doing any harm to William, has done him a service in lending him his plane for a year; for the same reason, he will do no harm to a second, a third, a fourth borrower, in the subsequent periods. Hence you may understand that the interest of a capital is as natural, as lawful, as useful, in the thousandth year, as in the first. We may go still further. It may happen that James lends more than a single plane. It is possible, that by means of working, of saving, of privations, of order, of activity, he may come to lend a multitude of planes and saws; that is to say, to do a multitude of services. I insist upon this point,--that if the first loan has been a social good, it will be the same with all the others; for they are all similar, and based upon the same principle. It may happen, then, that the amount of all the remunerations received by our honest operative, in exchange for services rendered by him, may suffice to maintain him. In this case, there will be a man in the world who has a right to live without working. I do not say that he would be doing right to give himself up to idleness--but I say, that he has a right to do so; and if he does so, it will be at nobody's expense, but quite the contrary. If society at all understands the nature of things, it will acknowledge that this man subsists on services which he receives certainly (as we all do), but which he lawfully receives in exchange for other services, which he himself has rendered, that he continues to render, and which are quite real, inasmuch as they are freely and voluntarily accepted.

And here we have a glimpse of one of the finest harmonies in the social world. I allude to leisure: not that leisure that the warlike and tyrannical classes arrange for themselves by the plunder of the workers, but that leisure which is the lawful and innocent fruit of past activity and economy. In expressing myself thus, I know that I shall shock many received ideas. But see! Is not leisure an essential spring in the social machine? Without it, the world would never have had a Newton, a Pascal, a Fenelon; mankind would have been ignorant of all arts, sciences, and of those wonderful inventions prepared originally by investigations of mere curiosity; thought would have been inert--man would have made no progress. On the other hand, if leisure could only be explained by plunder and oppression--if it were a benefit which could only be enjoyed unjustly, and at the expense of others, there would be no middle path between these two evils; either mankind would be reduced to the necessity of stagnating in a vegetable and stationary life, in eternal ignorance, from the absence of wheels to its machine--or else it would have to acquire these wheels at the price of inevitable injustice, and would necessarily present the sad spectacle, in one form or other, of the antique classification of human beings into masters and slaves. I defy any one to show me, in this case, any other alternative. We should be compelled to contemplate the Divine plan which governs society, with the regret of thinking that it presents a deplorable chasm. The stimulus of progress would be forgotten, or, which is worse, this stimulus would be no other than injustice itself. But no! God has not left such a chasm in His work of love. We must take care not to disregard His wisdom and power; for those whose imperfect meditations cannot explain the lawfulness of leisure, are very much like the astronomer who said, at a certain point in the heavens there ought to exist a planet which will be at last discovered, for without it the celestial world is not harmony, but discord.

Well, I say that, if well understood, the history of my humble plane, although very modest, is sufficient to raise us to the contemplation of one of the most consoling, but least understood of the social harmonies.

It is not true that we must choose between the denial or the unlawfulness of leisure; thanks to rent and its natural duration, leisure may arise from labour and saving. It is a pleasing prospect, which every one may have in view; a noble recompense, to which each may aspire. It makes its appearance in the world; it distributes itself proportionably to the exercise of certain virtues; it opens all the avenues to intelligence; it ennobles, it raises the morals; it spiritualizes the soul of humanity, not only without laying any weight on those of our brethren whose lot in life devotes them to severe labour, but relieving them gradually from the heaviest and most repugnant part of this labour. It is enough that capitals should be formed, accumulated, multiplied; should be lent on conditions less and less burdensome; that they should descend, penetrate into every social circle, and that by an admirable progression, after having liberated the lenders, they should hasten the liberation of the borrowers themselves. For that end, the laws and customs ought all to be favourable to economy, the source of capital. It is enough to say, that the first of all these conditions is, not to alarm, to attack, to deny that which is the stimulus of saving and the reason of its existence--interest.

As long as we see nothing passing from hand to hand, in the character of loan, but provisions, materials, instruments, things indispensable to the productiveness of labour itself, the ideas thus far exhibited will not find many opponents. Who knows, even, that I may not be reproached for having made a great effort to burst what may be said to be an open door. But as soon as cash makes its appearance as the subject of the transaction (and it is this which appears almost always), immediately a crowd of objections are raised. Money, it will be said, will not reproduce it self, like your sack of corn; it does not assist labour, like your plane; it does not afford an immediate satisfaction, like your house. It is incapable, by its nature, of producing interest, of multiplying itself, and the remuneration it demands is a positive extortion.

Who cannot see the sophistry of this? Who does not see that cash is only a transient form, which men give at the time to othervalues, to real objects of usefulness, for the sole object of facilitating their arrangements? In the midst of social complications, the man who is in a condition to lend, scarcely ever has the exact thing which the borrower wants. James, it is true, has a plane; but, perhaps, William wants a saw. They cannot negotiate; the transaction favourable to both cannot take place, and then what happens? It happens that James first exchanges his plane for money; he lends the money to William, and William exchanges the money for a saw. The transaction is no longer a simple one; it is decomposed into two parts, as I explained above in speaking of exchange. But, for all that, it has not changed its nature; it still contains all the elements of a direct loan. James has still got rid of a tool which was useful to him; William has still received an instrument which perfects his work and increases his profits; there is still a service rendered by the lender, which entitles him to receive an equivalent service from the borrower; this just balance is not the less established by free mutual bargaining. The very natural obligation to restore at the end of the term the entire value, still constitutes the principle of the duration of interest.

At the end of a year, says M. Thoré, will you find an additional crown in a bag of a hundred pounds?

No, certainly, if the borrower puts the bag of one hundred pounds on the shelf. In such a case, neither the plane nor the sack of corn would reproduce themselves. But it is not for the sake of leaving the money in the bag, nor the plane on the hook, that they are borrowed. The plane is borrowed to be used, or the money to procure a plane. And if it is clearly proved that this tool enables the borrower to obtain profits which he would not have made without it, if it is proved that the lender has renounced creating for himself this excess of profits, we may understand how the stipulation of a part of this excess of profits in favour of the lender, is equitable and lawful.

Ignorance of the true part which cash plays in human transactions, is the source of the most fatal errors. I intend devoting an entire pamphlet to this subject. From what we may infer from the writings of M. Proudhon, that which has led him to think that gratuitous credit was a logical and definite consequence of social progress, is the observation of the phenomenon which shows a decreasing interest, almost in direct proportion to the rate of civilisation. In barbarous times it is, in fact, cent, per cent., and more. Then it descends to eighty, sixty, fifty, forty, twenty, ten, eight, five, four, and three per cent. In Holland, it has even been as low as two per cent. Hence it is concluded, that "in proportion as society comes to perfection, it will descend to zero by the time civilisation is complete. In other words, that which characterises social perfection is the gratuitousness of credit. When, therefore, we shall have abolished interest, we shall have reached the last step of progress." This is mere sophistry, and as such false arguing may contribute to render popular the unjust, dangerous, and destructive dogma, that credit should be gratuitous, by representing it as coincident with social perfection, with the reader's permission I will examine in a few words this new view of the question.

What is interest? It is the service rendered, after a free bargain, by the borrower to the lender, in remuneration for the service he has received by the loan. By what law is the rate of these remunerative services established? By the general law which regulates the equivalent of all services; that is, by the law of supply and demand.

The more easily a thing is procured, the smaller is the service rendered by yielding it or lending it. The man who gives me a glass of water in the Pyrenees, does not render me so great a service as he who allows me one in the desert of Sahara. If there are many planes, sacks of corn, or houses, in a country, the use of them is obtained, other things being equal, on more favourable conditions than if they were few; for the simple reason, that the lender renders in this case a smaller relative service.

It is not surprising, therefore, that the more abundant capitals are, the lower is the interest.

Is this saying that it will ever reach zero? No; because, I repeat it, the principle of a remuneration is in the loan. To say that interest will be annihilated, is to say that there will never be any motive for saving, for denying ourselves, in order to form new capitals, nor even to preserve the old ones. In this case, the waste would immediately bring a void, and interest would directly reappear.

In that, the nature of the services of which we are speaking does not differ from any other. Thanks to industrial progress, a pair of stockings, which used to be worth six francs, has successively been worth only four, three, and two. No one can say to what point this value will descend; but we can affirm that it will never reach zero, unless the stockings finish by producing themselves spontaneously. Why? Because the principle of remuneration is in labour; because he who works for another renders a service, and ought to receive a service. If no one paid for stockings, they would cease to be made; and, with the scarcity, the price would not fail to reappear.

The sophism which I am now combating has its root in the infinite divisibility which belongs to value, as it does to matter.

It appears at first paradoxical, but it is well known to all mathematicians, that, through all eternity, fractions may be taken from a weight without the weight ever being annihilated. It is sufficient that each successive fraction be less than the preceding one, in a determined and regular proportion.

There are countries where people apply themselves to increasing the size of horses, or diminishing in sheep the size of the head. It is impossible to say precisely to what point they will arrive in this. No one can say that he has seen the largest horse or the smallest sheep's head that will ever appear in the world. But he may safely say that the size of horses will never attain to infinity, nor the heads of sheep to nothing.

In the same way, no one can say to what point the price of stockings nor the interest of capitals will come down; but we may safely affirm, when we know the nature of things, that neither the one nor the other will ever arrive at zero, for labour and capital can no more live without recompense than a sheep without a head.

The arguments of M. Proudhon reduce themselves, then, to this:--Since the most skilful agriculturists are those who have reduced the heads of sheep to the smallest size, we shall have arrived at the highest agricultural perfection when sheep have no longer any heads. Therefore, in order to realise the perfection, let us behead them.

I have now done with this wearisome discussion. Why is it that the breath of false doctrine has made it needful to examine into the intimate nature of interest? I must not leave off without remarking upon a beautiful moral which may be drawn from this law:--"The depression of interest is proportioned to the abundance of capitals." This law being granted, if there is a class of men to whom it is more important than to any other that capitals be formed, accumulate, multiply, abound, and superabound, it is certainly the class which borrows them directly or indirectly; it is those men who operate upon materials, who gain assistance by instruments, who live upon provisions, produced and economised by other men.

Imagine, in a vast and fertile country, a population of a thousand inhabitants, destitute of all capital thus defined. It will assuredly perish by the pangs of hunger. Let us suppose a case hardly less cruel. Let us suppose that ten of these savages are provided with instruments and provisions sufficient to work and to live themselves until harvest time, as well as to remunerate the services of eighty labourers. The inevitable result will be the death of nine hundred human beings. It is clear, then, that since 990 men, urged by want, will crowd upon the supports which would only maintain a hundred, the ten capitalists will be masters of the market. They will obtain labour on the hardest conditions, for they will put it up to auction, or the highest bidder. And observe this,--if these capitalists entertain such pious sentiments as would induce them to impose personal privations on themselves, in order to diminish the sufferings of some of their brethren, this generosity, which attaches to morality, will be as noble in its principle as useful in its effects. But if, duped by that false philosophy which persons wish so inconsiderately to mingle with economic laws, they take to remunerating labour largely, far from doing good, they will do harm. They will give double wages, it may be. But then, forty-five men will be better provided for, whilst forty-five others will come to augment the number of those who are sinking into the grave. Upon this supposition, it is not the lowering of wages which is the mischief, it is the scarcity of capital. Low wages are not the cause, but the effect of the evil. I may add, that they are to a certain extent the remedy. It acts in this way: it distributes the burden of suffering as much as it can, and saves as many lives as a limited quantity of sustenance permits.

Suppose now, that instead of ten capitalists, there should be a hundred, two hundred, five hundred,--is it not evident that the condition of the whole population, and, above all, that of the "prolétaires,"[3] will be more and more improved? Is it not evident that, apart from every consideration of generosity, they would obtain more work and better pay for it?--that they themselves will be in a better condition, to form capitals, without being able to fix the limits to this ever-increasing facility of realising equality and well-being? Would it not be madness in them to admit such doctrines, and to act in a way which would drain the source of wages, and paralyse the activity and stimulus of saving? Let them learn this lesson, then; doubtless, capitals are good for those who possess them: who denies it? But they are also useful to those who have not yet been able to form them; and it is important to those who have them not, that others should have them.

Yes, if the "prolétaires" knew their true interests, they would seek, with the greatest care, what circumstances are, and what are not favourable to saving, in order to favour the former and to discourage the latter. They would sympathise with every measure which tends to the rapid formation of capitals. They would be enthusiastic promoters of peace, liberty, order, security, the union of classes and peoples, economy, moderation in public expenses, simplicity in the machinery of government; for it is under the sway of all these circumstances that saving does its work, brings plenty within the reach of the masses, invites those persons to become the formers of capital who were formerly under the necessity of borrowing upon hard conditions. They would repel with energy the warlike spirit, which diverts from its true course so large a part of human labour; the monopolising spirit, which deranges the equitable distribution of riches, in the way by which liberty alone can realise it; the multitude of public services, which attack our purses only to check our liberty; and, in short, those subversive, hateful, thoughtless doctrines, which alarm capital, prevent its formation, oblige it to flee, and finally to raise its price, to the especial disadvantage of the workers, who bring it into operation. Well, and in this respect is not the revolution of February a hard lesson? Is it not evident that the insecurity it has thrown into the world of business on the one hand; and, on the other, the advancement of the fatal theories to which I have alluded, and which, from the clubs, have almost penetrated into the regions of the legislature, have everywhere raised the rate of interest? Is it not evident, that from that time the "prolétaires" have found greater difficulty in procuring those materials, instruments, and provisions, without which labour is impossible? Is it not that which has caused stoppages; and do not stoppages, in their turn, lower wages? Thus there is a deficiency of labour to the "prolétaires," from the same cause which loads the objects they consume with an increase of price, in consequence of the rise of interest. High interest, low wages, means in other words that the same article preserves its price, but that the part of the capitalist has invaded, without profiting himself, that of the workmen.

A friend of mine, commissioned to make inquiry into Parisian industry, has assured me that the manufacturers have revealed to him a very striking fact, which proves, better than any reasoning can, how much insecurity and uncertainty injure the formation of capital. It was remarked, that during the most distressing period, the popular expenses of mere fancy had not diminished. The small theatres, the fighting lists, the public-houses, and tobacco depots, were as much frequented as in prosperous times. In the inquiry, the operatives themselves explained this phenomenon thus:--"What is the use of pinching? Who knows what will happen to us? Who knows that interest will not be abolished? Who knows but that the State will become a universal and gratuitous lender, and that it will wish to annihilate all the fruits which we might expect from our savings?" Well! I say, that if such ideas could prevail during two single years, it would be enough to turn our beautiful France into a Turkey--misery would become general and endemic, and, most assuredly, the poor would be the first upon whom it would fall.

Workmen! they talk to you a great deal upon the artificial organisation of labour;--do you know why they do so? Because they are ignorant of the laws of its natural organisation; that is, of the wonderful organisation which results from liberty. You are told, that liberty gives rise to what is called the radical antagonism of classes; that it creates, and makes to clash, two opposite interests--that of the capitalists and that of the "prolétaires." But we ought to begin by proving that this antagonism exists by a law of nature; and afterwards it would remain to be shown how far the arrangements of restraint are superior to those of liberty, for between liberty and restraint I see no middle path. Again, it would remain to be proved that restraint would always operate to your advantage, and to the prejudice of the rich. But, no; this radical antagonism, this natural opposition of interests, does not exist. It is only an evil dream of perverted and intoxicated imaginations. No; a plan so defective has not proceeded from the Divine Mind. To affirm it, we must begin by denying the existence of God. And see how, by means of social laws, and because men exchange amongst themselves their labours and their productions, see what a harmonious tie attaches the classes one to the other! There are the landowners; what is their interest? That the soil be fertile, and the sun beneficent: and what is the result? That corn abounds, that it falls in price, and the advantage turns to the profit of those who have had no patrimony. There are the manufacturers--what is their constant thought? To perfect their labour, to increase the power of their machines, to procure for themselves, upon the best terms, the raw material. And to what does all this tend? To the abundance and the low price of produce; that is, that all the efforts of the manufacturers, and without their suspecting it, result in a profit to the public consumer, of which each of you is one. It is the same with every profession. Well, the capitalists are not exempt from this law. They are very busy making schemes, economising, and turning them to their advantage. This is all very well; but the more they succeed, the more do they promote the abundance of capital, and, as a necessary consequence, the reduction of interest. Now, who is it that profits by the reduction of interest? Is it not the borrower first, and finally, the consumers of the things which the capitals contribute to produce?

It is therefore certain that the final result of the efforts of each class is the common good of all.

You are told that capital tyrannises over labour. I do not deny that each one endeavours to draw the greatest possible advantage from his situation; but, in this sense, he realises only that which is possible. Now, it is never more possible for capitals to tyrannise over labour, than when they are scarce; for then it is they who make the law--it is they who regulate the rate of sale. Never is this tyranny more impossible to them, than when they are abundant; for, in that case, it is labour which has the command.

Away, then, with the jealousies of classes, ill-will, unfounded hatreds, unjust suspicions. These depraved passions injure those who nourish them in their hearts. This is no declamatory morality; it is a chain of causes and effects, which is capable of being rigorously, mathematically demonstrated. It is not the less sublime, in that it satisfies the intellect as well as the feelings.

I shall sum up this whole dissertation with these words:--Workmen, labourers, "prolétaires," destitute and suffering classes, will you improve your condition? You will not succeed by strife, insurrection, hatred, and error. But there are three things which cannot perfect the entire community, without extending these benefits to yourselves; these things are--peace, liberty, and security.

THAT WHICH IS SEEN, AND THAT WHICH IS NOT SEEN

In the department of economy, an act, a habit, an institution, a law, gives birth not only to an effect, but to a series of effects. Of these effects, the first only is immediate; it manifests itself simultaneously with its cause--it is seen. The others unfold in succession--they are not seen: it is well for us if they are foreseen. Between a good and a bad economist this constitutes the whole difference--the one takes account of the visible effect; the other takes account both of the effects which are seen and also of those which it is necessary to foresee. Now this difference is enormous, for it almost always happens that when the immediate consequence is favourable, the ultimate consequences are fatal, and the converse. Hence it follows that the bad economist pursues a small present good, which will be followed by a great evil to come, while the true economist pursues a great good to come, at the risk of a small present evil.

In fact, it is the same in the science of health, arts, and in that of morals. If often happens, that the sweeter the first fruit of a habit is, the more bitter are the consequences. Take, for example, debauchery, idleness, prodigality. When, therefore, a man, absorbed in the effect which is seen, has not yet learned to discern those which are not seen, he gives way to fatal habits, not only by inclination, but by calculation.

This explains the fatally grievous condition of mankind. Ignorance surrounds its cradle: then its actions are determined by their first consequences, the only ones which, in its first stage, it can see. It is only in the long run that it learns to take account of the others. It has to learn this lesson from two very different masters--experience and foresight. Experience teaches effectually, but brutally. It makes us acquainted with all the effects of an action, by causing us to feel them; and we cannot fail to finish by knowing that fire burns, if we have burned ourselves. For this rough teacher, I should like, if possible, to substitute a more gentle one. I mean Foresight. For this purpose I shall examine the consequences of certain economical phenomena, by placing in opposition to each other those which are seen, and those which are not seen.

I.--THE BROKEN WINDOW.

Have you ever witnessed the anger of the good shopkeeper, James B., when his careless son happened to break a pane of glass? If you have been present at such a scene, you will most assuredly bear witness to the fact, that every one of the spectators, were there even thirty of them, by common consent apparently, offered the unfortunate owner this invariable consolation--"It is an ill wind that blows nobody good. Everybody must live, and what would become of the glaziers if panes of glass were never broken?"

Now, this form of condolence contains an entire theory, which it will be well to show up in this simple case, seeing that it is precisely the same as that which, unhappily, regulates the greater part of our economical institutions.

Suppose it cost six francs to repair the damage, and you say that the accident brings six francs to the glazier's trade--that it encourages that trade to the amount of six francs--I grant it; I have not a word to say against it; you reason justly. The glazier comes, performs his task, receives his six francs, rubs his hands, and, in his heart, blesses the careless child. All this is that which is seen.

But if, on the other hand, you come to the conclusion, as is too often the case, that it is a good thing to break windows, that it causes money to circulate, and that the encouragement of industry in general will be the result of it, you will oblige me to call out, "Stop there! your theory is confined to that which is seen; it takes no account of that which is not seen."

It is not seen that as our shopkeeper has spent six francs upon one thing, he cannot spend them upon another. It is not seen that if he had not had a window to replace, he would, perhaps, have replaced his old shoes, or added another book to his library. In short, he would have employed his six francs in some way which this accident has prevented.

Let us take a view of industry in general, as affected by this circumstance. The window being broken, the glazier's trade is encouraged to the amount of six francs: this is that which is seen.

If the window had not been broken, the shoemaker's trade (or some other) would have been encouraged to the amount of six francs: this is that which is not seen.

And if that which is not seen is taken into consideration, because it is a negative fact, as well as that which is seen, because it is a positive fact, it will be understood that neither industry in general, nor the sum total of national labour, is affected, whether windows are broken or not.

Now let us consider James B. himself. In the former supposition, that of the window being broken, he spends six francs, and has neither more nor less than he had before, the enjoyment of a window.

In the second, where we suppose the window not to have been broken, he would have spent six francs in shoes, and would have had at the same time the enjoyment of a pair o shoes and of a window.

Now, as James B. forms a part of society, we must come to the conclusion, that, taking it altogether, and making an estimate of its enjoyments and its labours, it has lost the value of the broken window.

Whence we arrive at this unexpected conclusion: "Society loses the value of things which are uselessly destroyed;" and we must assent to a maxim which will make the hair of protectionists stand on end--To break, to spoil, to waste, is not to encourage national labour; or, more briefly, "destruction is not profit."

What will you say, Moniteur Industriel--what will you say, disciples of good M. F. Chamans, who has calculated with so much precision how much trade would gain by the burning of Paris, from the number of houses it would be necessary to rebuild?

I am sorry to disturb these ingenious calculations, as far as their spirit has been introduced into our legislation; but I beg him to begin them again, by taking into the account that which is not seen, and placing it alongside of that which is seen.

The reader must take care to remember that there are not two persons only, but three concerned in the little scene which I have submitted to his attention. One of them, James B., represents the consumer, reduced, by an act of destruction, to one enjoyment instead of two. Another, under the title of the glazier, shows us the producer, whose trade is encouraged by the accident. The third is the shoemaker (or some other tradesman), whose labour suffers proportionably by the same cause. It is this third person who is always kept in the shade, and who, personating that which is not seen, is a necessary element of the problem. It is he who shows us how absurd it is to think we see a profit in an act of destruction. It is he who will soon teach us that it is not less absurd to see a profit in a restriction, which is, after all, nothing else than a partial destruction. Therefore, if you will only go to the root of all the arguments which are adduced in its favour, all you will find will be the paraphrase of this vulgar saying--What would become of the glaziers, if nobody ever broke windows?

II.--THE DISBANDING OF TROOPS.

It is the same with a people as it is with a man. If it wishes to give itself some gratification, it naturally considers whether it is worth what it costs. To a nation, security is the greatest of advantages. If, in order to obtain it, it is necessary to have an army of a hundred thousand men, I have nothing to say against it. It is an enjoyment bought by a sacrifice. Let me not be misunderstood upon the extent of my position. A member of the assembly proposes to disband a hundred thousand men, for the sake of relieving the tax-payers of a hundred millions.

If we confine ourselves to this answer--"The hundred millions of men, and these hundred millions of money, are indispensable to the national security: it is a sacrifice; but without this sacrifice, France would be torn by factions or invaded by some foreign power,"--I have nothing to object to this argument, which may be true or false in fact, but which theoretically contains nothing which militates against economy. The error begins when the sacrifice itself is said to be an advantage because it profits somebody.

Now I am very much mistaken if, the moment the author of the proposal has taken his seat, some orator will not rise and say--"Disband a hundred thousand men! Do you know what you are saying? What will become of them? Where will they get a living? Don't you know that work is scarce everywhere? That every field is over-stocked? Would you turn them out of doors to increase competition and to weigh upon the rate of wages? Just now, when it is a hard matter to live at all, it would be a pretty thing if the State must find bread for a hundred thousand individuals? Consider, besides, that the army consumes wine, arms, clothing--that it promotes the activity of manufactures in garrison towns--that it is, in short, the godsend of innumerable purveyors. Why, any one must tremble at the bare idea of doing away with this immense industrial movement."

This discourse, it is evident, concludes by voting the maintenance of a hundred thousand soldiers, for reasons drawn from the necessity of the service, and from economical considerations. It is these considerations only that I have to refute.

A hundred thousand men, costing the tax-payers a hundred millions of money, live and bring to the purveyors as much as a hundred millions can supply. This is that which is seen.

But, a hundred millions taken from the pockets of the tax-payers, cease to maintain these tax-payers and the purveyors, as far as a hundred millions reach. This is that which is not seen. Now make your calculations. Cast up, and tell me what profit there is for the masses?

I will tell you where the loss lies; and to simplify it, instead of speaking of a hundred thousand men and a million of money, it shall be of one man and a thousand francs.

We will suppose that we are in the village of A. The recruiting sergeants go their round, and take off a man. The tax-gatherers go their round, and take off a thousand francs. The man and the sum of money are taken to Metz, and the latter is destined to support the former for a year without doing anything. If you consider Metz only, you are quite right; the measure is a very advantageous one: but if you look towards the village of A., you will judge very differently; for, unless you are very blind indeed, you will see that that village has lost a worker, and the thousand francs which would remunerate his labour, as well as the activity which, by the expenditure of those thousand francs, it would spread around it.

At first sight, there would seem to be some compensation. What took place at the village, now takes place at Metz, that is all. But the loss is to be estimated in this way:--At the village, a man dug and worked; he was a worker. At Metz, he turns to the right about and to the left about; he is a soldier. The money and the circulation are the same in both cases; but in the one there were three hundred days of productive labour, in the other there are three hundred days of unproductive labour, supposing, of course, that a part of the army is not indispensable to the public safety.

Now, suppose the disbanding to take place. You tell me there will be a surplus of a hundred thousand workers, that competition will be stimulated, and it will reduce the rate of wages. This is what you see.

But what you do not see is this. You do not see that to dismiss a hundred thousand soldiers is not to do away with a million of money, but to return it to the tax-payers. You do not see that to throw a hundred thousand workers on the market, is to throw into it, at the same moment, the hundred millions of money needed to pay for their labour: that, consequently, the same act which increases the supply of hands, increases also the demand; from which it follows, that your fear of a reduction of wages is unfounded. You do not see that, before the disbanding as well as after it, there are in the country a hundred millions of money corresponding with the hundred thousand men. That the whole difference consists in this: before the disbanding, the country gave the hundred millions to the hundred thousand men for doing nothing; and that after it, it pays them the same sum for working. You do not see, in short, that when a tax-payer gives his money either to a soldier in exchange for nothing, or to a worker in exchange for something, all the ultimate consequences of the circulation of this money are the same in the two cases; only, in the second case the tax-payer receives something, in the former he receives nothing. The result is--a dead loss to the nation.

The sophism which I am here combating will not stand the test of progression, which is the touchstone of principles. If, when every compensation is made, and all interests satisfied, there is a national profit in increasing the army, why not enrol under its banners the entire male population of the country?

III.--TAXES.

Have you never chanced to hear it said: "There is no better investment than taxes. Only see what a number of families it maintains, and consider how it reacts upon industry: it is an inexhaustible stream, it is life itself."

In order to combat this doctrine, I must refer to my preceding refutation. Political economy knew well enough that its arguments were not so amusing that it could be said of them, repetitions please. It has, therefore, turned the proverb to its own use, well convinced that, in its mouth, repetitions teach.

The advantages which officials advocate are those which are seen. The benefit which accrues to the providers is still that which is seen. This blinds all eyes.

But the disadvantages which the tax-payers have to get rid of are those which are not seen. And the injury which results from it to the providers is still that which is not seen, although this ought to be self-evident.

When an official spends for his own profit an extra hundred sous, it implies that a tax-payer spends for his profit a hundred sous less. But the expense of the official is seen, because the act is performed, while that of the tax-payer is not seen, because, alas! he is prevented from performing it.

You compare the nation, perhaps to a parched tract of land, and the tax to a fertilising rain. Be it so. But you ought also to ask yourself where are the sources of this rain, and whether it is not the tax itself which draws away the moisture from the ground and dries it up?

Again, you ought to ask yourself whether it is possible that the soil can receive as much of this precious water by rain as it loses by evaporation?

There is one thing very certain, that when James B. counts out a hundred sous for the tax-gatherer, he receives nothing in return. Afterwards, when an official spends these hundred sous, and returns them to James B., it is for an equal value in corn or labour. The final result is a loss to James B. of five francs.

It is very true that often, perhaps very often, the official performs for James B. an equivalent service. In this case there is no loss on either side; there is merely an exchange. Therefore, my arguments do not at all apply to useful functionaries. All I say is,--if you wish to create an office, prove its utility. Show that its value to James B., by the services which it performs for him, is equal to what it costs him. But, apart from this intrinsic utility, do not bring forward as an argument the benefit which it confers upon the official, his family, and his providers; do not assert that it encourages labour.

When James B. gives a hundred sous to a Government officer for a really useful service, it is exactly the same as when he gives a hundred sous to a shoemaker for a pair of shoes.

But when James B. gives a hundred sous to a Government officer, and receives nothing for them unless it be annoyances, he might as well give them to a thief. It is nonsense to say that the Government officer will spend these hundred sous to the great profit ofnational labour; the thief would do the same; and so would James B., if he had not been stopped on the road by the extra-legal parasite, nor by the lawful sponger.

Let us accustom ourselves, then, to avoid judging of things by what is seen only, but to judge of them by that which is not seen.

Last year I was on the Committee of Finance, for under the constituency the members of the Opposition were not systematically excluded from all the Commissions: in that the constituency acted wisely. We have heard M. Thiers say--"I have passed my life in opposing the legitimist party and the priest party. Since the common danger has brought us together, now that I associate with them and know them, and now that we speak face to face, I have found out that they are not the monsters I used to imagine them."

Yes, distrust is exaggerated, hatred is fostered among parties who never mix; and if the majority would allow the minority to be present at the Commissions, it would perhaps be discovered that the ideas of the different sides are not so far removed from each other; and, above all, that their intentions are not so perverse as is supposed. However, last year I was on the Committee of Finance. Every time that one of our colleagues spoke of fixing at a moderate figure the maintenance of the President of the Republic, that of the ministers, and of the ambassadors, it was answered:--

"For the good of the service, it is necessary to surround certain offices with splendour and dignity, as a means of attracting men of merit to them. A vast number of unfortunate persons apply to the President of the Republic, and it would be placing him in a very painful position to oblige him to be constantly refusing them. A certain style in the ministerial saloons is a part of the machinery of constitutional Governments."

Although such arguments may be controverted, they certainly deserve a serious examination. They are based upon the public interest, whether rightly estimated or not; and as far as I am concerned, I have much more respect for them than many of our Catos have, who are actuated by a narrow spirit of parsimony or of jealousy.

But what revolts the economical part of my conscience, and makes me blush for the intellectual resources of my country, is when this absurd relic of feudalism is brought forward, which it constantly is, and it is favourably received too:--

"Besides, the luxury of great Government officers encourages the arts, industry, and labour. The head of the State and his ministers cannot give banquets and soirées without causing life to circulate through all the veins of the social body. To reduce their means, would starve Parisian industry, and consequently that of the whole nation."

I must beg you, gentlemen, to pay some little regard to arithmetic, at least; and not to say before the National Assembly in France, lest to its shame it should agree with you, that an addition gives a different sum, according to whether it is added up from the bottom to the top, or from the top to the bottom of the column.

For instance, I want to agree with a drainer to make a trench in my field for a hundred sous. Just as we have concluded our arrangement the tax-gatherer comes, takes my hundred sous, and sends them to the Minister of the Interior; my bargain is at end, but the minister will have another dish added to his table. Upon what ground will you dare to affirm that this official expense helps the national industry? Do you not see, that in this there is only a reversing of satisfaction and labour? A minister has his table better covered, it is true; but it is just as true that an agriculturist has his field worse drained. A Parisian tavern-keeper has gained a hundred sous, I grant you; but then you must grant me that a drainer has been prevented from gaining five francs. It all comes to this,--that the official and the tavern-keeper being satisfied, is that which is seen; the field undrained, and the drainer deprived of his job, is that which is not seen. Dear me! how much trouble there is in proving that two and two make four; and if you succeed in proving it, it is said "the thing is so plain it is quite tiresome," and they vote as if you had proved nothing at all.

IV.--THEATRES, FINE ARTS.

Ought the State to support the arts?

There is certainly much to be said on both sides of this question. It may be said, in favour of the system of voting supplies for this purpose, that the arts enlarge, elevate, and harmonize the soul of a nation; that they divert it from too great an absorption in material occupations; encourage in it a love for the beautiful; and thus act favourably on its manners, customs, morals, and even on its industry. It may be asked, what would become of music in France without her Italian theatre and her Conservatoire; of the dramatic art, without her Théâtre-Français; of painting and sculpture, without our collections, galleries, and museums? It might even be asked, whether, without centralisation, and consequently the support of the fine arts, that exquisite taste would be developed which is the noble appendage of French labour, and which introduces its productions to the whole world? In the face of such results, would it not be the height of imprudence to renounce this moderate contribution from all her citizens, which, in fact, in the eyes of Europe, realises their superiority and their glory?

To these and many other reasons, whose force I do not dispute, arguments no less forcible may be opposed. It might first of all be said, that there is a question of distributive justice in it. Does the right of the legislator extend to abridging the wages of the artisan, for the sake of, adding to the profits of the artist? M. Lamartine said, "If you cease to support the theatre, where will you stop? Will you not necessarily be led to withdraw your support from your colleges, your museums, your institutes, and your libraries? It might be answered, if you desire to support everything which is good and useful, where will you stop? Will you not necessarily be led to form a civil list for agriculture, industry, commerce, benevolence, education? Then, is it certain that Government aid favours the progress of art? This question is far from being settled, and we see very well that the theatres which prosper are those which depend upon their own resources. Moreover, if we come to higher considerations, we may observe that wants and desires arise the one from the other, and originate in regions which are more and more refined in proportion as the public wealth allows of their being satisfied; that Government ought not to take part in this correspondence, because in a certain condition of present fortune it could not by taxation stimulate the arts of necessity without checking those of luxury, and thus interrupting the natural course of civilisation. I may observe, that these artificial transpositions of wants, tastes, labour, and population, place the people in a precarious and dangerous position, without any solid basis."

These are some of the reasons alleged by the adversaries of State intervention in what concerns the order in which citizens think their wants and desires should be satisfied, and to which, consequently, their activity should be directed. I am, I confess, one of those who think that choice and impulse ought to come from below and not from above, from the citizen and not from the legislator; and the opposite doctrine appears to me to tend to the destruction of liberty and of human dignity.

But, by a deduction as false as it is unjust, do you know what economists are accused of? It is, that when we disapprove of government support, we are supposed to disapprove of the thing itself whose support is discussed; and to be the enemies of every kind of activity, because we desire to see those activities, on the one hand free, and on the other seeking their own reward in themselves. Thus, if we think that the State should not interfere by taxation in religious affairs, we are atheists. If we think the State ought not to interfere by taxation in education, we are hostile to knowledge. If we say that the State ought not by taxation to give a fictitious value to land, or to any particular branch of industry, we are enemies to property and labour. If we think that the State ought not to support artists, we are barbarians, who look upon the arts as useless.

Against such conclusions as these I protest with all my strength. Far from entertaining the absurd idea of doing away with religion, education, property, labour, and the arts, when we say that the State ought to protect the free development of all these kinds of human activity, without helping some of them at the expense of others--we think, on the contrary, that all these living powers of society would develop themselves more harmoniously under the influence of liberty; and that, under such an influence no one of them would, as is now the case, be a source of trouble, of abuses, of tyranny, and disorder.

Our adversaries consider that an activity which is neither aided by supplies, nor regulated by government, is an activity destroyed. We think just the contrary. Their faith is in the legislator, not in mankind; ours is in mankind, not in the legislator.

Thus M. Lamartine said, "Upon this principle we must abolish the public exhibitions, which are the honour and the wealth of this country." But I would say to M. Lamartine,--According to your way of thinking, not to support is to abolish; because, setting out upon the maxim that nothing exists independently of the will of the State, you conclude that nothing lives but what the State causes to live. But I oppose to this assertion the very example which you have chosen, and beg you to remark, that the grandest and noblest of exhibitions, one which has been conceived in the most liberal and universal spirit--and I might even make use of the term humanitary, for it is no exaggeration--is the exhibition now preparing in London; the only one in which no government is taking any part, and which is being paid for by no tax.

To return to the fine arts. There are, I repeat, many strong reasons to be brought, both for and against the system of government assistance. The reader must see that the especial, object of this work leads me neither to explain these reasons, nor to decide in their favour, nor against them.

But M. Lamartine has advanced one argument which I cannot pass by in silence, for it is closely connected with this economic study. "The economical question, as regards theatres, is comprised in one word--labour. It matters little what is the nature of this labour; it is as fertile, as productive a labour as any other kind of labour in the nation. The theatres in France, you know, feed and salary no less than 80,000 workmen of different kinds; painters, masons, decorators, costumers, architects, &c., which constitute the very life and movement of several parts of this capital, and on this account they ought to have your sympathies." Your sympathies! say rather your money.

And further on he says: "The pleasures of Paris are the labour and the consumption of the provinces, and the luxuries of the rich are the wages and bread of 200,000 workmen of every description, who live by the manifold industry of the theatres on the surface of the republic, and who receive from these noble pleasures, which render France illustrious, the sustenance of their lives and the necessaries of their families and children. It is to them that you will give 60,000 francs." (Very well; very well. Great applause.) For my part I am constrained to say, "Very bad! very bad!" confining this opinion, of course, within the bounds of the economical question which we are discussing.

Yes, it is to the workmen of the theatres that a part, at least, of these 60,000 francs will go; a few bribes, perhaps, may be abstracted on the way. Perhaps, if we were to look a little more closely into the matter, we might find that the cake had gone another way, and that those workmen were fortunate who had come in for a few crumbs. But I will allow, for the sake of argument, that the entire sum does go to the painters, decorators, &c.

This is that which is seen. But whence does it come? This is the other side of the question, and quite as important as the former. Where do these 60,000 francs spring from? and where would they go, if a vote of the legislature did not direct them first towards the Rue Rivoli and thence towards the Rue Grenelle? This is what is not seen. Certainly, nobody will think of maintaining that the legislative vote has caused this sum to be hatched in a ballot urn; that it is a pure addition made to the national wealth; that but for this miraculous vote these 60,000 francs would have been for ever invisible and impalpable. It must be admitted that all that the majority can do is to decide that they shall be taken from one place to be sent to another; and if they take one direction, it is only because they have been diverted from another.

This being the case, it is clear that the tax-payer, who has contributed one franc, will no longer have this franc at his own disposal. It is clear that he will be deprived of some gratification to the amount of one franc; and that the workman, whoever he may be, who would have received it from him, will be deprived of a benefit to that amount. Let us not, therefore, be led by a childish illusion into believing that the vote of the 60,000 francs may add anything whatever to the well-being of the country, and to national labour. It displaces enjoyments, it transposes wages--that is all.

Will it be said that for one kind of gratification, and one kind of labour, it substitutes more urgent, more moral, more reasonable gratifications and labour? I might dispute this; I might say, by taking 60,000 francs from the tax-payers, you diminish the wages of labourers, drainers, carpenters, blacksmiths, and increase in proportion those of the singers.

There is nothing to prove that this latter class calls for more sympathy than the former. M. Lamartine does not say that it is so. He himself says that the labour of the theatres is as fertile, as productive as any other (not more so); and this may be doubted; for the best proof that the latter is not so fertile as the former lies in this, that the other is to be called upon to assist it.

But this comparison between the value and the intrinsic merit of different kinds of labour forms no part of my present subject. All I have to do here is to show, that if M. Lamartine and those persons who commend his line of argument have seen on one side the salaries gained by the providers of the comedians, they ought on the other to have seen the salaries lost by the providers of the taxpayers: for want of this, they have exposed themselves to ridicule by mistaking a displacement for a gain. If they were true to their doctrine, there would be no limits to their demands for government aid; for that which is true of one franc and of 60,000 is true, under parallel circumstances, of a hundred millions of francs.

When taxes are the subject of discussion, you ought to prove their utility by reasons from the root of the matter, but not by this unlucky assertion--"The public expenses support the working classes." This assertion disguises the important fact, that public expenses always supersede private expenses, and that therefore we bring a livelihood to one workman instead of another, but add nothing to the share of the working class as a whole. Your arguments are fashionable enough, but they are too absurd to be justified by anything like reason.

V.--PUBLIC WORKS.

Nothing is more natural than that a nation, after having assured itself that an enterprise will benefit the community, should have it executed by means of a general assessment. But I lose patience, I confess, when I hear this economic blunder advanced in support of such a project--"Besides, it will be a means of creating labour for the workmen."

The State opens a road, builds a palace, straightens a street, cuts a canal, and so gives work to certain workmen--this is what is seen: but it deprives certain other workmen of work--and this is what is not seen.

The road is begun. A thousand workmen come every morning, leave every evening, and take their wages--this is certain. If the road had not been decreed, if the supplies had not been voted, these good people would have had neither work nor salary there; this also is certain.

But is this all? Does not the operation, as a whole, contain something else? At the moment when M. Dupin pronounces the emphatic words, "The Assembly has adopted," do the millions descend miraculously on a moonbeam into the coffers of MM. Fould and Bineau? In order that the evolution may be complete, as it is said, must not the State organise the receipts as well as the expenditure? must it not set its tax-gatherers and tax-payers to work, the former to gather and the latter to pay?

Study the question, now, in both its elements. While you state the destination given by the State to the millions voted, do not neglect to state also the destination which the tax-payer would have given, but cannot now give, to the same. Then you will understand that a public enterprise is a coin with two sides. Upon one is engraved a labourer at work, with this device, that which is seen; on the other is a labourer out of work, with the device, that which is not seen.

The sophism which this work is intended to refute is the more dangerous when applied to public works, inasmuch as it serves to justify the most wanton enterprises and extravagance. When a railroad or a bridge are of real utility, it is sufficient to mention this utility. But if it does not exist, what do they do? Recourse is had to this mystification: "We must find work for the workmen."

Accordingly, orders are given that the drains in the Champ-de-Mars be made and unmade. The great Napoleon, it is said, thought he was doing a very philanthropic work by causing ditches to be made and then filled up. He said, therefore, "What signifies the result? All we want is to see wealth spread among the labouring classes."

But let us go to the root of the matter. We are deceived by money. To demand the co-operation of all the citizens in a common work, in the form of money, is in reality to demand a concurrence in kind; for every one procures, by his own labour, the sum to which he is taxed. Now, if all the citizens were to be called together, and made to execute, in conjunction, a work useful to all, this would be easily understood; their reward would be found in the results of the work itself.

But after having called them together, if you force them to make roads which no one will pass through, palaces which no one will inhabit, and this under the pretext of finding them work, it would be absurd, and they would have a right to argue, "With this labour we have nothing to do; we prefer working on our own account."

A proceeding which consists in making the citizens co-operate in giving money but not labour, does not, in any way, alter the general results. The only thing is, that the loss would react upon all parties. By the former, those whom the State employs, escape their part of the loss, by adding it to that which their fellow-citizens have already suffered.

There is an article in our constitution which says:--"Society favours and encourages the development of labour--by the establishment of public works, by the State, the departments, and the parishes, as a means of employing persons who are in want of work."

As a temporary measure, on any emergency, during a hard winter, this interference with the tax-payers may have its use. It acts in the same way as securities. It adds nothing either to labour or to wages, but it takes labour and wages from ordinary times to give them, at a loss it is true, to times of difficulty.

As a permanent, general, systematic measure, it is nothing else than a ruinous mystification, an impossibility, which shows a little excited labour which is seen, and hides a great deal of prevented labour which is not seen.

VI.--THE INTERMEDIATES.

Society is the total of the forced or voluntary services which men perform for each other; that is to say, of public services and private services.

The former, imposed and regulated by the law, which it is not always easy to change, even when it is desirable, may survive with it their own usefulness, and still preserve the name of public services, even when they are no longer services at all, but rather public annoyances. The latter belong to the sphere of the will, of individual responsibility. Every one gives and receives what he wishes, and what he can, after a debate. They have always the presumption of real utility, in exact proportion to their comparative value.

This is the reason why the former description of services so often become stationary, while the latter obey the law of progress.

While the exaggerated development of public services, by the waste of strength which it involves, fastens upon society a fatal sycophancy, it is a singular thing that several modern sects, attributing this character to free and private services, are endeavouring to transform professions into functions.

These sects violently oppose what they call intermediates. They would gladly suppress the capitalist, the banker, the speculator, the projector, the merchant, and the trader, accusing them of interposing between production and consumption, to extort from both, without giving either anything in return. Or rather, they would transfer to the State the work which they accomplish, for this work cannot be suppressed.

The sophism of the Socialists on this point is, showing to the public what it pays to the intermediates in exchange for their services, and concealing from it what is necessary to be paid to the State. Here is the usual conflict between what is before our eyes and what is perceptible to the mind only; between what is seen and what is not seen.

It was at the time of the scarcity, in 1847, that the Socialist schools attempted and succeeded in popularizing their fatal theory. They knew very well that the most absurd notions have always a chance with people who are suffering; malisunda fames.

Therefore, by the help of the fine words, "trafficking in men by men, speculation on hunger, monopoly," they began to blacken commerce, and to cast a veil over its benefits.

"What can be the use," they say, "of leaving to the merchants the care of importing food from the United States and the Crimea? Why do not the State, the departments, and the towns, organize a service for provisions and a magazine for stores? They would sell at a return price, and the people, poor things, would be exempted from the tribute which they pay to free, that is, to egotistical, individual, and anarchical commerce."

The tribute paid by the people to commerce is that which is seen. The tribute which the people would pay to the State, or to its agents, in the Socialist system, is what is not seen.

In what does this pretended tribute, which the people pay to commerce, consist? In this: that two men render each other a mutual service, in all freedom, and under the pressure of competition and reduced prices.

When the hungry stomach is at Paris, and corn which can satisfy it is at Odessa, the suffering cannot cease till the corn is brought into contact with the stomach. There are three means by which this contact may be effected. 1st. The famished men may go themselves and fetch the corn. 2nd. They may leave this task to those to whose trade it belongs. 3rd. They may club together, and give the office in charge to public functionaries. Which of these three methods possesses the greatest advantages? In every time, in all countries, and the more free, enlightened, and experienced they are, men have voluntarily chosen the second. I confess that this is sufficient, in my opinion, to justify this choice. I cannot believe that mankind, as a whole, is deceiving itself upon a point which touches it so nearly. But let us now consider the subject.

For thirty-six millions of citizens to go and fetch the corn they want from Odessa, is a manifest impossibility. The first means, then, goes for nothing. The consumers cannot act for themselves. They must, of necessity, have recourse to intermediates, officials or agents.

But observe, that the first of these three means would be the most natural. In reality, the hungry man has to fetch his corn. It is a task which concerns himself, a service due to himself. If another person, on whatever ground, performs this service for him, takes the task upon himself, this latter has a claim upon him for a compensation. I mean by this to say that intermediates contain in themselves the principle of remuneration.

However that may be, since we must refer to what the Socialists call a parasite, I would ask, which of the two is the most exacting parasite the merchant or the official?

Commerce (free, of course, otherwise I could not reason upon it), commerce, I say, is led by its own interests to study the seasons, to give daily statements of the state of the crops, to receive information from every part of the globe, to foresee wants, to take precautions beforehand. It has vessels always ready, correspondents everywhere; and it is its immediate interest to buy at the lowest possible price, to economize in all the details of its operations, and to attain the greatest results by the smallest efforts. It is not the French merchants only who are occupied in procuring provisions for France in time of need, and if their interest leads them irresistibly to accomplish their task at the smallest possible cost, the competition which they create amongst each other leads them no less irresistibly to cause the consumers to partake of the profits of those realised savings. The corn arrives: it is to the interest of commerce to sell it as soon as possible, so as to avoid risks, to realise its funds, and begin again the first opportunity.

Directed by the comparison of prices, it distributes food over the whole surface of the country, beginning always at the highest, price, that is, where the demand is the greatest. It is impossible to imagine an organisation more completely calculated to meet the interest of those who are in want; and the beauty of this organisation, unperceived as it is by the Socialists, results from the very fact that it is free. It is true, the consumer is obliged to reimburse commerce for the expenses of conveyance, freight, store-room, commission, &c.; but can any system be devised in which he who eats corn is not obliged to defray the expenses, whatever they may be, of bringing it within his reach? The remuneration for the service performed has to be paid also; but as regards its amount, this is reduced to the smallest possible sum by competition; and as regards its justice, it would be very strange if the artizans of Paris would not work for the artizans of Marseilles, when the merchants of Marseilles work for the artizans of Paris.

If, according to the Socialist invention, the State were to stand in the stead of commerce, what would happen? I should like to be informed where the saving would be to the public? Would it be in the price of purchase? Imagine the delegates of 40,000 parishes arriving at Odessa on a given day, and on the day of need: imagine the effect upon prices. Would the saving be in the expenses? Would fewer vessels be required; fewer sailors, fewer transports, fewer sloops? or would you be exempt from the payment of all these things? Would it be in the profits of the merchants? Would your officials go to Odessa for nothing? Would they travel and work on the principle of fraternity? Must they not live? Must not they be paid for their time? And do you believe that these expenses would not exceed a thousand times the two or three per cent. which the merchant gains, at the rate at which he is ready to treat?

And then consider the difficulty of levying so many taxes, and of dividing so much food. Think of the injustice, of the abuses inseparable from such an enterprise. Think of the responsibility which would weigh upon the Government.

The Socialists who have invented these follies, and who, in the days of distress, have introduced them into the minds of the masses, take to themselves literally the title of advanced men; and it is not without some danger that custom, that tyrant of tongues, authorizes the term, and the sentiment which it involves. Advanced! This supposes that these gentlemen can see further than the common people; that their only fault is that they are too much in advance of their age; and if the time is not yet come for suppressing certain free services, pretended parasites, the fault is to be attributed to the public which is in the rear of Socialism. I say, from my soul and my conscience, the reverse is the truth; and I know not to what barbarous age we should have to go back, if we would find the level of Socialist knowledge on this subject. These modern sectarians incessantly oppose association to actual society. They overlook the fact that society, under a free regulation, is a true association, far superior to any of those which proceed from their fertile imaginations.

Let me illustrate this by an example. Before a mutual services, and to helping each other in a common object, and that all may be considered, with respect to others, intermediates. If, for instance, in the course of the operation, the conveyance becomes important enough to occupy one person, the spinning another, the weaving another, why should the first be considered a parasitemore than the other two? The conveyance must be made, must it not? Does not he who performs it devote to it his time and trouble? and by so doing does he not spare that of his colleagues? Do these do more or other than this for him? Are they not equally dependent for remuneration, that is, for the division of the produce, upon the law of reduced price? Is it not in all liberty, for the common good, that this separation of work takes place, and that these arrangements are entered into? What do we want with a Socialist then, who, under pretence of organising for us, comes despotically to break up our voluntary arrangements, to check the division of labour, to substitute isolated efforts for combined ones, and to send civilisation back? Is association, as I describe it here, in itself less association, because every one enters and leaves it freely, chooses his place in it, judges and bargains for himself on his own responsibility, and brings with him the spring and warrant of personal interest? That it may deserve this name, is it necessary that a pretended reformer should come and impose upon us his plan and his will, and, as it were, to concentrate mankind in himself?

The more we examine these advanced schools, the more do we become convinced that there is but one thing at the root of them: ignorance proclaiming itself infallible, and claiming despotism in the name of this infallibility.

I hope the reader will excuse this digression. It may not be altogether useless, at a time when declamations, springing from St. Simonian, Phalansterian, and Icarian books, are invoking the press and the tribune, and which seriously threaten the liberty of labour and commercial transactions.

VII.--RESTRICTIONS.

M. Prohibant (it was not I who gave him this name, but M. Charles Dupin) devoted his time and capital to converting the ore found on his land into iron. As nature had been more lavish towards the Belgians, they furnished the French with iron cheaper than M. Prohibant; which means, that all the French, or France, could obtain a given quantity of iron with less labour by buying it of the honest Flemings. Therefore, guided by their own interest, they did not fail to do so; and every day there might be seen a multitude of nail-smiths, blacksmiths, cartwrights, machinists, farriers, and labourers, going themselves, or sending intermediates, to supply themselves in Belgium. This displeased M. Prohibant exceedingly.

At first, it occurred to him to put an end to this abuse by his own efforts: it was the least he could do, for he was the only sufferer. "I will take my carbine," said he; "I will put four pistols into my belt; I will fill my cartridge box; I will gird on my sword, and go thus equipped to the frontier. There, the first blacksmith, nail-smith, farrier, machinist, or locksmith, who presents himself to do his own business and not mine, I will kill, to teach him how to live." At the moment of starting, M. Prohibant made a few reflections which calmed down his warlike ardour a little. He said to himself, "In the first place, it is not absolutely impossible that the purchasers of iron, my countrymen and enemies, should take the thing ill, and, instead of letting me kill them, should kill me instead; and then, even were I to call out all my servants, we should not be able to defend the passages. In short, this proceeding would cost me very dear, much more so than the result would be worth."

M. Prohibant was on the point of resigning himself to his sad fate, that of being only as free as the rest of the world, when a ray of light darted across his brain. He recollected that at Paris there is a great manufactory of laws. "What is a law?" said he to himself. "It is a measure to which, when once it is decreed, be it good or bad, everybody is bound to conform. For the execution of the same a public force is organised, and to constitute the said public force, men and money are drawn from the whole nation. If, then, I could only get the great Parisian manufactory to pass a little law, 'Belgian iron is prohibited,' I should obtain the following results:--The Government would replace the few valets that I was going to send to the frontier by 20,000 of the sons of those refractory blacksmiths, farriers, artizans, machinists, locksmiths, nail-smiths, and labourers. Then to keep these 20,000 custom-house officers in health and good humour, it would distribute among them 25,000,000 of francs taken from these blacksmiths, nail-smiths, artizans, and labourers. They would guard the frontier much better; would cost me nothing; I should not be exposed to the brutality of the brokers; should sell the iron at my own price, and have the sweet satisfaction of seeing our great people shamefully mystified. That would teach them to proclaim themselves perpetually the harbingers and promoters of progress in Europe. Oh! it would be a capital joke, and deserves to be tried."

So M. Prohibant went to the law manufactory. Another time, perhaps, I shall relate the story of his underhand dealings, but now I shall merely mention his visible proceedings. He brought the following consideration before the view of the legislating gentlemen.

"Belgian iron is sold in France at ten francs, which obliges me to sell mine at the same price. I should like to sell at fifteen, but cannot do so on account of this Belgian iron, which I wish was at the bottom of the Red Sea. I beg you will make a law that no more Belgian iron shall enter France. Immediately I raise my price five francs, and these are the consequences:--

"For every hundred-weight of iron that I shall deliver to the public, I shall receive fifteen francs instead of ten; I shall grow rich more rapidly, extend my traffic, and employ more workmen. My workmen and I shall spend much more freely, to the great advantage of our tradesmen for miles around. These latter, having more custom, will furnish more employment to trade, and activity on both sides will increase in the country. This fortunate piece of money, which you will drop into my strong-box, will, like a stone thrown into a lake, give birth to an infinite number of concentric circles."

Charmed with his discourse, delighted to learn that it is so easy to promote, by legislating, the prosperity of a people, the law-makers voted the restriction. "Talk of labour and economy," they said, "what is the use of these painful means of increasing the national wealth, when all that is wanted for this object is a decree?"

And, in fact, the law produced all the consequences announced by M. Prohibant: the only thing was, it produced others which he had not foreseen. To do him justice, his reasoning was not false, but only incomplete. In endeavouring to obtain a privilege, he had taken cognizance of the effects which are seen, leaving in the background those which are not seen. He had pointed out only two personages, whereas there are three concerned in the affair. It is for us to supply this involuntary or premeditated omission.

It is true, the crown-piece, thus directed by law into M. Prohibant's strong-box, is advantageous to him and to those whose labour it would encourage; and if the Act had caused the crown-piece to descend from the moon, these good effects would not have been counterbalanced by any corresponding evils. Unfortunately, the mysterious piece of money does not come from the moon, but from the pocket of a blacksmith, or a nail-smith, or a cartwright, or a farrier, or a labourer, or a shipwright; in a word, from James B., who gives it now without receiving a grain more of iron than when he was paying ten francs. Thus, we can see at a glance that this very much alters the state of the case; for it is very evident that M. Prohibant's profit is compensated by James B.'s loss, and all that M. Prohibant can do with the crown-piece, for the encouragement of national labour, James B. might have done himself. The stone has only been thrown upon one part of the lake, because the law has prevented it from being thrown upon another.

Therefore, that which is not seen supersedes that which is seen, and at this point there remains, as the residue of the operation, a piece of injustice, and, sad to say, a piece of injustice perpetrated by the law!

This is not all. I have said that there is always a third person left in the background. I must now bring him forward, that he may reveal to us a second loss of five francs. Then we shall have the entire results of the transaction.

James B. is the possessor of fifteen francs, the fruit of his labour. He is now free. What does he do with his fifteen francs? He purchases some article of fashion for ten francs, and with it he pays (or the intermediate pay for him) for the hundred-weight of Belgian iron. After this he has five francs left. He does not throw them into the river, but (and this is what is not seen) he gives them to some tradesman in exchange for some enjoyment; to a bookseller, for instance, for Bossuet's "Discourse on Universal History."

Thus, as far as national labour is concerned, it is encouraged to the amount of fifteen francs, viz.:--ten francs for the Paris article, five francs to the bookselling trade.

As to James B., he obtains for his fifteen francs two gratifications, viz.:--

1st. A hundred-weight of iron.

2nd. A book.

The decree is put in force. How does it affect the condition of James B.? How does it affect the national labour?

James B. pays every centime of his five francs to M. Prohibant, and therefore is deprived of the pleasure of a book, or of some other thing of equal value. He loses five francs. This must be admitted; it cannot fail to be admitted, that when the restriction raises the price of things, the consumer loses the difference.

But, then, it is said, national labour is the gainer.

No, it is not the gainer; for since the Act, it is no more encouraged than it was before, to the amount of fifteen francs.

The only thing is that, since the Act, the fifteen francs of James B. go to the metal trade, while before it was put in force, they were divided between the milliner and the bookseller.

The violence used by M. Prohibant on the frontier, or that which he causes to be used by the law, may be judged very differently in a moral point of view. Some persons consider that plunder is perfectly justifiable, if only sanctioned by law. But, for myself, I cannot imagine anything more aggravating. However it may be, the economical results are the same in both cases.

Look at the thing as you will; but if you are impartial, you will see that no good can come of legal or illegal plunder. We do not deny that it affords M. Prohibant, or his trade, or, if you will, national industry, a profit of five francs. But we affirm that it causes two losses, one to James B., who pays fifteen francs where he otherwise would have paid ten; the other to national industry, which does not receive the difference. Take your choice of these two losses, and compensate with it the profit which we allow. The other will prove not the less a dead loss. Here is the moral: To take by violence is not to produce, but to destroy. Truly, if taking by violence was producing, this country of ours would be a little richer than she is.

VIII.--MACHINERY.

"A curse on machines! Every year, their increasing power devotes millions of workmen to pauperism, by depriving them of work, and therefore of wages and bread. A curse on machines!"

This is the cry which is raised by vulgar prejudice, and echoed in the journals.

But to curse machines is to curse the spirit of humanity!

It puzzles me to conceive how any man can feel any satisfaction in such a doctrine.

For, if true, what is its inevitable consequence? That there is no activity, prosperity, wealth, or happiness possible for any people, except for those who are stupid and inert, and to whom God has not granted the fatal gift of knowing how to think, to observe, to combine, to invent, and to obtain the greatest results with the smallest means. On the contrary, rags, mean huts, poverty, and inanition, are the inevitable lot of every nation which seeks and finds in iron, fire, wind, electricity, magnetism, the laws of chemistry and mechanics, in a word, in the powers of nature, an assistance to its natural powers. We might as well say with Rousseau--"Every man that thinks is a depraved animal."

This is not all. If this doctrine is true, since all men think and invent, since all, from first to last, and at every moment of their existence, seek the co-operation of the powers of nature, and try to make the most of a little, by reducing either the work of their hands or their expenses, so as to obtain the greatest possible amount of gratification with the smallest possible amount of labour, it must follow, as a matter of course, that the whole of mankind is rushing towards its decline, by the same mental aspiration towards progress, which torments each of its members.

Hence, it ought to be made known, by statistics, that the inhabitants of Lancashire, abandoning that land of machines, seek for work in Ireland, where they are unknown; and, by history, that barbarism darkens the epochs of civilisation, and that civilisation shines in times of ignorance and barbarism.

There is evidently in this mass of contradictions something which revolts us, and which leads us to suspect that the problem contains within it an element of solution which has not been sufficiently disengaged.

Here is the whole mystery: behind that which is seen lies something which is not seen. I will endeavour to bring it to light. The demonstration I shall give will only be a repetition of the preceding one, for the problems are one and the same.

Men have a natural propensity to make the best bargain they can, when not prevented by an opposing force; that is, they like to obtain as much as they possibly can for their labour, whether the advantage is obtained from a foreign producer or a skilfulmechanical producer.

The theoretical objection which is made to this propensity is the same in both cases. In each case it is reproached with the apparent inactivity which it causes to labour. Now, labour rendered available, not inactive, is the very thing which determines it. And, therefore, in both cases, the same practical obstacle--force, is opposed to it also.

The legislator prohibits foreign competition, and forbids mechanical competition. For what other means can exist for arresting a propensity which is natural to all men, but that of depriving them of their liberty?

In many countries, it is true, the legislator strikes at only one of these competitions, and confines himself to grumbling at the other. This only proves one thing, that is, that the legislator is inconsistent.

We need not be surprised at this. On a wrong road, inconsistency is inevitable; if it were not so, mankind would be sacrificed. A false principle never has been, and never will be, carried out to the end.

Now for our demonstration, which shall not be a long one.

James B. had two francs which he had gained by two workmen; but it occurs to him that an arrangement of ropes and weights might be made which would diminish the labour by half. Therefore he obtains the same advantage, saves a franc, and discharges a workman.

He discharges a workman: this is that which is seen.

And seeing this only, it is said, "See how misery attends civilisation; this is the way that liberty is fatal to equality. The human mind has made a conquest, and immediately a workman is cast into the gulf of pauperism. James B. may possibly employ the two workmen, but then he will give them only half their wages, for they will compete with each other, and offer themselves at the lowest price. Thus the rich are always growing richer, and the poor, poorer. Society wants remodelling." A very fine conclusion, and worthy of the preamble.

Happily, preamble and conclusion are both false, because, behind the half of the phenomenon which is seen, lies the other half which is not seen.

The franc saved by James B. is not seen, no more are the necessary effects of this saving.

Since, in consequence of his invention, James B. spends only one franc on hand labour in the pursuit of a determined advantage, another franc remains to him.

If, then, there is in the world a workman with unemployed arms, there is also in the world a capitalist with an unemployed franc. These two elements meet and combine, and it is as clear as daylight, that between the supply and demand of labour, and between the supply and demand of wages, the relation is in no way changed.

The invention and the workman paid with the first franc, now perform the work which was formerly accomplished by two workmen. The second workman, paid with the second franc, realises a new kind of work.

What is the change, then, which has taken place? An additional national advantage has been gained; in other words, the invention is a gratuitous triumph--a gratuitous profit for mankind.

From the form which I have given to my demonstration, the following inference might be drawn:--

"It is the capitalist who reaps all the advantage from machinery. The working class, if it suffers only temporarily, never profits by it, since, by your own showing, they displace a portion of the national labour, without diminishing it, it is true, but also without increasing it."

I do not pretend, in this slight treatise, to answer every objection; the only end I have in view, is to combat a vulgar, widely spread, and dangerous prejudice. I want to prove that a new machine only causes the discharge of a certain number of hands, when the remuneration which pays them is abstracted by force. These hands and this remuneration would combine to produce what it was impossible to produce before the invention; whence it follows, that the final result is an increase of advantages for equal labour.

Who is the gainer by these additional advantages?

First, it is true, the capitalist, the inventor; the first who succeeds in using the machine; and this is the reward of his genius and courage. In this case, as we have just seen, he effects a saving upon the expense of production, which, in whatever way it may be spent (and it always is spent), employs exactly as many hands as the machine caused to be dismissed.

But soon competition obliges him to lower his prices in proportion to the saving itself; and then it is no longer the inventor who reaps the benefit of the invention--it is the purchaser of what is produced, the consumer, the public, including the workman; in a word, mankind.

And that which is not seen is, that the saving thus procured for all consumers creates a fund whence wages may be supplied, and which replaces that which the machine has exhausted.

Thus, to recur to the forementioned example, James B. obtains a profit by spending two francs in wages. Thanks to his invention, the hand labour costs him only one franc. So long as he sells the thing produced at the same price, he employs one workman less in producing this particular thing, and that is what is seen; but there is an additional workman employed by the franc which James B. has saved. This is that which is not seen.

When, by the natural progress of things, James B. is obliged to lower the price of the thing produced by one franc, then he no longer realises a saving; then he has no longer a franc to dispose of to procure for the national labour a new production. But then another gainer takes his place, and this gainer is mankind. Whoever buys the thing he has produced, pays a franc less, and necessarily adds this saving to the fund of wages; and this, again, is what is not seen.

Another solution, founded upon facts, has been given of this problem of machinery.

It was said, machinery reduces the expense of production, and lowers the price of the thing produced. The reduction of the profit causes an increase of consumption, which necessitates an increase of production; and, finally, the introduction of as many workmen, or more, after the invention as were necessary before it. As a proof of this, printing, weaving, &c., are instanced.

This demonstration is not a scientific one. It would lead us to conclude, that if the consumption of the particular production of which we are speaking remains stationary, or nearly so, machinery must injure labour. This is not the case.

Suppose that in a certain country all the people wore hats. If, by machinery, the price could be reduced half, it would not necessarily follow that the consumption would be doubled.

Would you say that in this case a portion of the national labour had been paralyzed? Yes, according to the vulgar demonstration; but, according to mine, No; for even if not a single hat more should be bought in the country, the entire fund of wages would not be the less secure. That which failed to go to the hat-making trade would be found to have gone to the economy realised by all the consumers, and would thence serve to pay for all the labour which the machine had rendered useless, and to excite a new development of all the trades. And thus it is that things go on. I have known newspapers to cost eighty francs, now we pay forty-eight: here is a saving of thirty-two francs to the subscribers. It is not certain, or at least necessary, that the thirty-two francs should take the direction of the journalist trade; but it is certain, and necessary too, that if they do not take this direction they will take another. One makes use of them for taking in more newspapers; another, to get better living; another, better clothes; another, better furniture. It is thus that the trades are bound together. They form a vast whole, whose different parts communicate by secret canals: what is saved by one, profits all. It is very important for us to understand that savings never take place at the expense of labour and wages.

IX.--CREDIT.

In all times, but more especially of late years, attempts have been made to extend wealth by the extension of credit.

I believe it is no exaggeration to say, that since the revolution of February, the Parisian presses have issued more than 10,000 pamphlets, crying up this solution of the social problem.

The only basis, alas! of this solution, is an optical delusion--if, indeed, an optical delusion can be called a basis at all.

The first thing done is to confuse cash with produce, then paper money with cash; and from these two confusions it is pretended that a reality can be drawn.

It is absolutely necessary in this question to forget money, coin, bills, and the other instruments by means of which productions pass from hand to hand. Our business is with the productions themselves, which are the real objects of the loan; for when a farmer borrows fifty francs to buy a plough, it is not, in reality, the fifty francs which are lent to him, but the plough; and when a merchant borrows 20,000 francs to purchase a house, it is not the 20,000 francs which he owes, but the house. Money only appears for the sake of facilitating the arrangements between the parties.

Peter may not be disposed to lend his plough, but James may be willing to lend his money. What does William do in this case? He borrows money of James, and with this money he buys the plough of Peter.

But, in point of fact, no one borrows money for the sake of the money itself; money is only the medium by which to obtain possession of productions. Now, it is impossible in any country to transmit from one person to another more productions than that country contains.

Whatever may be the amount of cash and of paper which is in circulation, the whole of the borrowers cannot receive more ploughs, houses, tools, and supplies of raw material, than the lenders altogether can furnish; for we must take care not to forget that every borrower supposes a lender, and that what is once borrowed implies a loan.

This granted, what advantage is there in institutions of credit? It is, that they facilitate, between borrowers and lenders, the means of finding and treating with each other; but it is not in their power to cause an instantaneous increase of the things to be borrowed and lent. And yet they ought to be able to do so, if the aim of the reformers is to be attained, since they aspire to nothing less than to place ploughs, houses, tools, and provisions in the hands of all those who desire them.

And how do they intend to effect this?

By making the State security for the loan.

Let us try and fathom the subject, for it contains something which is seen, and also something which is not seen. We must endeavour to look at both.

We will suppose that there is but one plough in the world, and that two farmers apply for it.

Peter is the possessor of the only plough which is to be had in France; John and James wish to borrow it. John, by his honesty, his property, and good reputation, offers security. He inspires confidence; he has credit. James inspires little or no confidence. It naturally happens that Peter lends his plough to John.

But now, according to the Socialist plan, the State interferes, and says to Peter, "Lend your plough to James, I will be security for its return, and this security will be better than that of John, for he has no one to be responsible for him but himself; and I, although it is true that I have nothing, dispose of the fortune of the tax-payers, and it is with their money that, in case of need, I shall pay you the principal and interest." Consequently, Peter lends his plough to James: this is what is seen.

And the Socialists rub their hands, and say, "See how well our plan has answered. Thanks to the intervention of the State, poor James has a plough. He will no longer be obliged to dig the ground; he is on the road to make a fortune. It is a good thing for him, and an advantage to the nation as a whole."

Indeed, it is no such thing; it is no advantage to the nation, for there is something behind which is not seen.

It is not seen, that the plough is in the hands of James, only because it is not in those of John.

It is not seen, that if James farms instead of digging, John will be reduced to the necessity of digging instead of farming.

That, consequently, what was considered an increase of loan, is nothing but a displacement of loan. Besides, it is not seen that this displacement implies two acts of deep injustice.

It is an injustice to John, who, after having deserved and obtained credit by his honesty and activity, sees himself robbed of it.

It is an injustice to the tax-payers, who are made to pay a debt which is no concern of theirs.

Will any one say, that Government offers the same facilities to John as it does to James? But as there is only one plough to be had, two cannot be lent. The argument always maintains that, thanks to the intervention of the State, more will be borrowed than there are things to be lent; for the plough represents here the bulk of available capitals.

It is true, I have reduced the operation to the most simple expression of it, but if you submit the most complicated Government institutions of credit to the same test, you will be convinced that they can have but one result; viz., to displace credit, not to augment it. In one country, and in a given time, there is only a certain amount of capital available, and all are employed. In guaranteeing the non-payers, the State may, indeed, increase the number of borrowers, and thus raise the rate of interest (always to the prejudice of the tax-payer), but it has no power to increase the number of lenders, and the importance of the total of the loans.

There is one conclusion, however, which I would not for the world be suspected of drawing. I say, that the law ought not to favour, artificially, the power of borrowing, but I do not say that it ought not to restrain them artificially. If, in our system of mortgage, or in any other, there be obstacles to the diffusion of the application of credit, let them be got rid of; nothing can be better or more just than this. But this is all which is consistent with liberty, and it is all that any who are worthy of the name of reformers will ask.

X.--ALGERIA.

Here are four orators disputing for the platform. First, all the four speak at once; then they speak one after the other. What have they said? Some very fine things, certainly, about the power and the grandeur of France; about the necessity of sowing, if we would reap; about the brilliant future of our gigantic colony; about the advantage of diverting to a distance the surplus of our population, &c. &c. Magnificent pieces of eloquence, and always adorned with this conclusion:--"Vote fifty millions, more or less, for making ports and roads in Algeria; for sending emigrants thither; for building houses and breaking up land. By so doing, you will relieve the French workman, encourage African labour, and give a stimulus to the commerce of Marseilles. It would be profitable every way."

Yes, it is all very true, if you take no account of the fifty millions until the moment when the State begins to spend them; if you only see where they go, and not whence they come; if you look only at the good they are to do when they come out of the tax-gatherer's bag, and not at the harm which has been done, and the good which has been prevented, by putting them into it. Yes, at this limited point of view, all is profit. The house which is built in Barbary is that which is seen; the harbour made in Barbary is that which is seen; the work caused in Barbary is what is seen; a few less hands in France is what is seen; a great stir with goods at Marseilles is still that which is seen.

But, besides all this, there is something which is not seen. The fifty millions expended by the State cannot be spent, as they otherwise would have been, by the tax-payers. It is necessary to deduct, from all the good attributed to the public expenditure which has been effected, all the harm caused by the prevention of private expense, unless we say that James B. would have done nothing with the crown that he had gained, and of which the tax had deprived him; an absurd assertion, for if he took the trouble to earn it, it was because he expected the satisfaction of using it. He would have repaired the palings in his garden, which he cannot now do, and this is that which is not seen. He would have manured his field, which now he cannot do, and this is what is not seen. He would have added another story to his cottage, which he cannot do now, and this is what is not seen. He might have increased the number of his tools, which he cannot do now, and this is what is not seen. He would have been better fed, better clothed, have given a better education to his children, and increased his daughter's marriage portion; this is what is not seen. He would have become a member of the Mutual Assistance Society, but now he cannot; this is what is not seen. On one hand, are the enjoyments of which he has been deprived, and the means of action which have been destroyed in his hands; on the other, are the labour of the drainer, the carpenter, the smith, the tailor, the village schoolmaster, which he would have encouraged, and which are now prevented--all this is what is not seen.

Much is hoped from the future prosperity of Algeria; be it so. But the drain to which France is being subjected ought not to be kept entirely out of sight. The commerce of Marseilles is pointed out to me; but if this is to be brought about by means of taxation, I shall always show that an equal commerce is destroyed thereby in other parts of the country. It is said, "There is an emigrant transported into Barbary; this is a relief to the population which remains in the country," I answer, "How can that be, if, in transporting this emigrant to Algiers, you also transport two or three times the capital which would have served to maintain him in France?"4

The only object I have in view is to make it evident to the reader, that in every public expense, behind the apparent benefit, there is an evil which it is not so easy to discern. As far as in me lies, I would make him form a habit of seeing both, and taking account of both.

When a public expense is proposed, it ought to be examined in itself, separately from the pretended encouragement of labour which results from it, for tins encouragement is a delusion. Whatever is done in this way at the public expense, private expense would have done all the same; therefore, the interest of labour is always out of the question.

It is not the object of this treatise to criticise the intrinsic merit of the public expenditure as applied to Algeria, but I cannot withhold a general observation. It is, that the presumption is always unfavourable to collective expenses by way of tax. Why? For this reason:--First, justice always suffers from it in some degree. Since James B. had laboured to gain his crown, in the hope of receiving a gratification from it, it is to be regretted that the exchequer should interpose, and take from James B. this gratification, to bestow it upon another. Certainly, it behoves the exchequer, or those who regulate it, to give good reasons for this. It has been shown that the State gives a very provoking one, when it says, "With this crown I shall employ workmen;" for James B. (as soon as he sees it) will be sure to answer, "It is all very fine, but with this crown I might employ them myself."

Apart from this reason, others present themselves without disguise, by which the debate between the exchequer and poor James becomes much simplified. If the State says to him, "I take your crown to pay the gendarme, who saves you the trouble of providing for your own personal safety; for paving the street which you are passing through every day; for paying the magistrate who causes your property and your liberty to be respected; to maintain the soldier who maintains our frontiers,"--James B., unless I am much mistaken, will pay for all this without hesitation. But if the State were to say to him, "I take this crown that I may give you a little prize in case you cultivate your field well; or that I may teach your son something that you have no wish that he should learn; or that the Minister may add another to his score of dishes at dinner; I take it to build a cottage in Algeria, in which case I must take another crown every year to keep an emigrant in it, and another hundred to maintain a soldier to guard this emigrant, and another crown to maintain a general to guard this soldier," &c., &c.,--I think I hear poor James exclaim, "This system of law is very much like a system of cheat!" The State foresees the objection, and what does it do? It jumbles all things together, and brings forward just that provoking reason which ought to have nothing whatever to do with the question. It talks of the effect of this crown upon labour; it points to the cook and purveyor of the Minister; it shows an emigrant, a soldier, and a general, living upon the crown; it shows, in fact, what is seen, and if James B. has not learned to take into the account what is not seen, James B. will be duped. And this is why I want to do all I can to impress it upon his mind, by repeating it over and over again.

As the public expenses displace labour without increasing it, a second serious presumption presents itself against them. To displace labour is to displace labourers, and to disturb the natural laws which regulate the distribution of the population over the country. If 50,000,000 francs are allowed to remain in the possession of the tax-payers since the tax-payers are everywhere, they encourage labour in the 40,000 parishes in France. They act like a natural tie, which keeps every one upon his native soil; they distribute themselves amongst all imaginable labourers and trades. If the State, by drawing off these 60,000,000 francs from the citizens, accumulates them, and expends them on some given point, it attracts to this point a proportional quantity of displaced labour, a corresponding number of labourers, belonging to other parts; a fluctuating population, which is out of its place, and I venture to say dangerous when the fund is exhausted. Now here is the consequence (and this confirms all I have said): this feverish activity is, as it were, forced into a narrow space; it attracts the attention of all; it is what is seen. The people applaud; they are astonished at the beauty and facility of the plan, and expect to have it continued and extended. That which they do not see is, that an equal quantity of labour, which would probably be more valuable, has been paralyzed over the rest of France.

XI.--FRUGALITY AND LUXURY.

It is not only in the public expenditure that what is seen eclipses what is not seen. Setting aside what relates to political economy, this phenomenon leads to false reasoning. It causes nations to consider their moral and their material interests as contradictory to each other. What can be more discouraging or more dismal?

For instance, there is not a father of a family who does not think it his duty to teach his children order, system, the habits of carefulness, of economy, and of moderation in spending money.

There is no religion which does not thunder against pomp and luxury. This is as it should be; but, on the other hand, how frequently do we hear the following remarks:--

"To hoard, is to drain the veins of the people."

"The luxury of the great is the comfort of the little."

"Prodigals ruin themselves, but they enrich the State."

"It is the superfluity of the rich which makes bread for the poor."

Here, certainly, is a striking contradiction between the moral and the social idea. How many eminent spirits, after having made the assertion, repose in peace. It is a thing I never could understand, for it seems to me that nothing can be more distressing than to discover two opposite tendencies in mankind. Why, it comes to degradation at each of the extremes: economy brings it to misery; prodigality plunges it into moral degradation. Happily, these vulgar maxims exhibit economy and luxury in a false light, taking account, as they do, of those immediate consequences which are seen, and not of the remote ones, which are not seen. Let us see if we can rectify this incomplete view of the case.

Mondor and his brother Aristus, after dividing the parental inheritance, have each an income of 50,000 francs. Mondor practises the fashionable philanthropy. He is what is called a squanderer of money. He renews his furniture several times a year; changes his equipages every month. People talk of his ingenious contrivances to bring them sooner to an end: in short, he surpasses the fast livers of Balzac and Alexander Dumas.

Thus everybody is singing his praises. It is, "Tell us about Mondor! Mondor for ever! He is the benefactor of the workman; a blessing to the people. It is true, he revels in dissipation; he splashes the passers-by; his own dignity and that of human nature are lowered a little; but what of that? He does good with his fortune, if not with himself. He causes money to circulate; he always sends the tradespeople away satisfied. Is not money made round that it may roll?"

Aristus has adopted a very different plan of life. If he is not an egotist, he is, at any rate, an individualist, for he considers expense, seeks only moderate and reasonable enjoyments, thinks of his children's prospects, and, in fact, he economises.

And what do people say of him? "What is the good of a rich fellow like him? He is a skinflint. There is something imposing, perhaps, in the simplicity of his life; and he is humane, too, and benevolent, and generous, but he calculates. He does not spend his income; his house is neither brilliant nor bustling. What good does he do to the paper-hangers, the carriage makers, the horse dealers, and the confectioners?"

These opinions, which are fatal to morality, are founded upon what strikes the eye:--the expenditure of the prodigal; and another, which is out of sight, the equal and even superior expenditure of the economist.

But things have been so admirably arranged by the Divine inventor of social order, that in this, as in everything else, political economy and morality, far from clashing, agree; and the wisdom of Aristus is not only more dignified, but still more profitable, than the folly of Mondor. And when I say profitable, I do not mean only profitable to Aristus, or even to society in general, but more profitable to the workmen themselves--to the trade of the time.

To prove it, it is only necessary to turn the mind's eye to those hidden consequences of human actions, which the bodily eye does not see.

Yes, the prodigality of Mondor has visible effects in every point of view. Everybody can see his landaus, his phaetons, his berlins, the delicate paintings on his ceilings, his rich carpets, the brilliant effects of his house. Every one knows that his horses run upon the turf. The dinners which he gives at the Hotel de Paris attract the attention of the crowds on the Boulevards; and it is said, "That is a generous man; far from saving his income, he is very likely breaking into his capital." That is what is seen.

It is not so easy to see, with regard to the interest of workers, what becomes of the income of Aristus. If we were to trace it carefully, however, we should see that the whole of it, down to the last farthing, affords work to the labourers, as certainly as the fortune of Mondor. Only there is this difference: the wanton extravagance of Mondor is doomed to be constantly decreasing, and to come to an end without fail; whilst the wise expenditure of Aristus will go on increasing from year to year. And if this is the case, then, most assuredly, the public interest will be in unison with morality.

Aristus spends upon himself and his household 20,000 francs a year. If that is not sufficient to content him, he does not deserve to be called a wise man. He is touched by the miseries which oppress the poorer classes; he thinks he is bound in conscience to afford them some relief, and therefore he devotes 10,000 francs to acts of benevolence. Amongst the merchants, the manufacturers, and the agriculturists, he has friends who are suffering under temporary difficulties; he makes himself acquainted with their situation, that he may assist them with prudence and efficiency, and to this work he devotes 10,000 francs more. Then he does not forget that he has daughters to portion, and sons for whose prospects it is his duty to provide, and therefore he considers it a duty to lay by and put out to interest 10,000 francs every year.

The following is a list of his expenses:--

1st, Personal expenses 20,000 fr. 2nd, Benevolent objects 10,000 3rd, Offices of friendship 10,000 4th, Saving 10,000

Let us examine each of these items, and we shall see that not a single farthing escapes the national labour.

1st. Personal expenses.--These, as far as workpeople and tradesmen are concerned, have precisely the same effect as an equal sum spent by Mondor. This is self-evident, therefore we shall say no more about it.

2nd. Benevolent objects.--The 10,000 francs devoted to this purpose benefit trade in an equal degree; they reach the butcher, the baker, the tailor, and the carpenter. The only thing is, that the bread, the meat, and the clothing are not used by Aristus, but by those whom he has made his substitutes. Now, this simple substitution of one consumer for another in no way affects trade in general. It is all one, whether Aristus spends a crown or desires some unfortunate person to spend it instead.

3rd. Offices of friendship.--The friend to whom Aristus lends or gives 10,000 francs does not receive them to bury them; that would be against the hypothesis. He uses them to pay for goods, or to discharge debts. In the first case, trade is encouraged. Will any one pretend to say that it gains more by Mondor's purchase of a thoroughbred horse for 10,000 francs than by the purchase of 10,000 francs' worth of stuffs by Aristus or his friend? For if this sum serves to pay a debt, a third person appears, viz., the creditor, who will certainly employ them upon something in his trade, his household, or his farm. He forms another medium between Aristus and the workmen. The names only are changed, the expense remains, and also the encouragement to trade.

4th. Saving.--There remains now the 10,000 francs saved; and it is here, as regards the encouragement to the arts, to trade, labour, and the workmen, that Mondor appears far superior to Aristus, although, in a moral point of view, Aristus shows himself, in some degree, superior to Mondor.

I can never look at these apparent contradictions between the great laws of nature without a feeling of physical uneasiness which amounts to suffering. Were mankind reduced to the necessity of choosing between two parties, one of whom injures his interest, and the other his conscience, we should have nothing to hope from the future. Happily, this is not the case; and to see Aristus regain his economical superiority, as well as his moral superiority, it is sufficient to understand this consoling maxim, which is no less true from having a paradoxical appearance, "To save is to spend."

What is Aristus's object in saving 10,000 francs? Is it to bury them in his garden? No, certainly; he intends to increase his capital and his income; consequently, this money, instead of being employed upon his own personal gratification, is used for buying land, a house, &c., or it is placed in the hands of a merchant or a banker. Follow the progress of this money in any one of these cases, and you will be convinced, that through the medium of vendors or lenders, it is encouraging labour quite as certainly as if Aristus, following the example of his brother, had exchanged it for furniture, jewels, and horses.

For when Aristus buys lands or rents for 10,000 francs, he is determined by the consideration that he does not want to spend this money. This is why you complain of him.

But, at the same time, the man who sells the land or the rent, is determined by the consideration that he does want to spend the 10,000 francs in some way; so that the money is spent in any case, either by Aristus or by others in his stead.

With respect to the working class, to the encouragement of labour, there is only one difference between the conduct of Aristus and that of Mondor. Mondor spends the money himself, and around him, and therefore the effect is seen. Aristus, spending it partly through intermediate parties, and at a distance, the effect is not seen. But, in fact, those who know how to attribute effects to their proper causes, will perceive, that what is not seen is as certain as what is seen. This is proved by the fact, that in both cases the money circulates, and does not lie in the iron chest of the wise man, any more than it does in that of the spendthrift. It is, therefore, false to say that economy does actual harm to trade; as described above, it is equally beneficial with luxury.

But how far superior is it, if, instead of confining our thoughts to the present moment, we let them embrace a longer period!

Ten years pass away. What is become of Mondor and his fortune and his great popularity? Mondor is ruined. Instead of spending 60,000 francs every year in the social body, he is, perhaps, a burden to it. In any case, he is no longer the delight of shopkeepers; he is no longer the patron of the arts and of trade; he is no longer of any use to the workmen, nor are his successors, whom he has brought to want.

At the end of the same ten years Aristus not only continues to throw his income into circulation, but he adds an increasing sum from year to year to his expenses. He enlarges the national capital, that is, the fund which supplies wages, and as it is upon the extent of this fund that the demand for hands depends, he assists in progressively increasing the remuneration of the working class; and if he dies, he leaves children whom he has taught to succeed him in this work of progress and civilization.

In a moral point of view, the superiority of frugality over luxury is indisputable. It is consoling to think that it is so in political economy, to every one who, not confining his views to the immediate effects of phenomena, knows how to extend his investigations to their final effects.

XII.--HE WHO HAS A RIGHT TO WORK HAS A RIGHT TO PROFIT.

"Brethren, you must club together to find me work at your own price." This is the right to work; i.e., elementary socialism of the first degree.

"Brethren, you must club together to find me work at my own price." This is the right to profit; i.e., refined socialism, or socialism of the second degree.

Both of these live upon such of their effects as are seen. They will die by means of those effects which are not seen.

That which is seen is the labour and the profit excited by social combination. That which is not seen is the labour and the profit to which this same combination would give rise, if it were left to the tax-payers.

In 1848, the right to labour for a moment showed two faces. This was sufficient to ruin it in public opinion.

One of these faces was called national workshops. The other, forty-five centimes. Millions of francs went daily from the Rue Rivoli to the national workshops. This was the fair side of the medal.

And this is the reverse. If millions are taken out of a cash-box, they must first have been put into it. This is why the organisers of the right to public labour apply to the tax-payers.

Now, the peasants said, "I must pay forty-five centimes; then I must deprive myself of some clothing. I cannot manure my field; I cannot repair my house."

And the country workmen said, "As our townsman deprives himself of some clothing, there will be less work for the tailor; as he does not improve his field, there will be less work for the drainer; as he does not repair his house, there will be less work for the carpenter and mason."

It was then proved that two kinds of meal cannot come out of one sack, and that the work furnished by the Government was done at the expense of labour, paid for by the tax-payer. This was the death of the right to labour, which showed itself as much a chimera as an injustice. And yet, the right to profit, which is only an exaggeration of the right to labour, is still alive and flourishing.

Ought not the protectionist to blush at the part he would make society play?

He says to it, "You must give me work, and, more than that, lucrative work. I have foolishly fixed upon a trade by which I lose ten per cent. If you impose a tax of twenty francs upon my countrymen, and give it to me, I shall be a gainer instead of a loser. Now, profit is my right; you owe it me." Now, any society which would listen to this sophist, burden itself with taxes to satisfy him, and not perceive that the loss to which any trade is exposed is no less a loss when others are forced to make up for it,--such a society, I say, would deserve the burden inflicted upon it.

Thus we learn by the numerous subjects which I have treated, that, to be ignorant of political economy is to allow ourselves to be dazzled by the immediate effect of a phenomenon; to be acquainted with it is to embrace in thought and in forethought the whole compass of effects.

I might subject a host of other questions to the same test; but I shrink from the monotony of a constantly uniform demonstration, and I conclude by applying to political economy what Chateaubriand says of history:--

"There are," he says, "two consequences in history; an immediate one, which is instantly recognized, and one in the distance, which is not at first perceived. These consequences often contradict each other; the former are the results of our own limited wisdom, the latter, those of that wisdom which endures. The providential event appears after the human event. God rises up behind men. Deny, if you will, the supreme counsel; disown its action; dispute about words; designate, by the term, force of circumstances, or reason, what the vulgar call Providence; but look to the end of an accomplished fact, and you will see that it has always produced the contrary of what was expected from it, if it was not established at first upon morality and justice."--Chateaubriand's Posthumous Memoirs.

GOVERNMENT.

I wish some one would offer a prize--not of a hundred francs, but of a million, with crowns, medals and ribbons--for a good, simple and intelligible definition of the word "Government."

What an immense service it would confer on society!

The Government! what is it? where is it? what does it do? what ought it to do? All we know is, that it is a mysterious personage; and, assuredly, it is the most solicited, the most tormented, the most overwhelmed, the most admired, the most accused, the most invoked, and the most provoked, of any personage in the world.

I have not the pleasure of knowing my reader, but I would stake ten to one, that for six months he has been making Utopias, and if so, that he is looking to Government for the realization of them.

And should the reader happen to be a lady, I have no doubt that she is sincerely desirous of seeing all the evils of suffering humanity remedied, and that she thinks this might easily be done, if Government would only undertake it.

But, alas! that poor unfortunate personage, like Figaro, knows not to whom to listen, nor where to turn. The hundred thousand mouths of the press and of the platform cry out all at once:--

"Organize labour and workmen.

"Do away with egotism.

"Repress insolence and the tyranny of capital.

"Make experiments upon manure and eggs.

"Cover the country with railways.

"Irrigate the plains.

"Plant the hills.

"Make model farms.

"Found social workshops.

"Colonize Algeria.

"Suckle children.

"Instruct the youth.

"Assist the aged.

"Send the inhabitants of towns into the country.

"Equalize the profits of all trades.

"Lend money without interest to all who wish to borrow."

"Emancipate Italy, Poland, and Hungary."

"Rear and perfect the saddle-horse."

"Encourage the arts, and provide us with musicians and dancers."

"Restrict commerce, and at the same time create a merchant navy."

"Discover truth, and put a grain of reason into our heads. The mission of Government is to enlighten, to develop, to extend, to fortify, to spiritualize, and to sanctify the soul of the people."

"Do have a little patience, gentlemen," says Government in a beseeching tone. "I will do what I can to satisfy you, but for this I must have resources. I have been preparing plans for five or six taxes, which are quite new, and not at all oppressive. You will see how willingly people will pay them."

Then comes a great exclamation:--"No! indeed! where is the merit of doing a thing with resources? Why, it does not deserve the name of a Government! So far from loading us with fresh taxes, we would have you withdraw the old ones. You ought to suppress

"The salt tax,

"The tax on liquors,

"The tax on letters,

"Custom-house duties,

"Patents."

In the midst of this tumult, and now that the country has two or three times changed its Government, for not having satisfied all its demands, I wanted to show that they were contradictory. But what could I have been thinking about? Could I not keep this unfortunate observation to myself?

I have lost my character for ever! I am looked upon as a man without heart and without feeling--a dry philosopher, an individualist, a plebeian--in a word, an economist of the English or American school. But, pardon me, sublime writers, who stop at nothing, not even at contradictions. I am wrong, without a doubt, and I would willingly retract. I should be glad enough, you may be sure, if you had really discovered a beneficent and inexhaustible being, calling itself the Government, which has bread for all mouths, work for all hands, capital for all enterprises, credit for all projects, oil for all wounds, balm for all sufferings, advice for all perplexities, solutions for all doubts, truths for all intellects, diversions for all who want them, milk for infancy, and wine for old age--which can provide for all our wants, satisfy all our curiosity, correct all our errors, repair all our faults, and exempt us henceforth from the necessity for foresight, prudence, judgment, sagacity, experience, order, economy, temperance and activity.

What reason could I have for not desiring to see such a discovery made? Indeed, the more I reflect upon it, the more do I see that nothing could be more convenient than that we should all of us have within our reach an inexhaustible source of wealth and enlightenment--a universal physician, an unlimited treasure, and an infallible counsellor, such as you describe Government to be. Therefore it is that I want to have it pointed out and defined, and that a prize should be offered to the first discoverer of the phœnix. For no one would think of asserting that this precious discovery has yet been made, since up to this time everything presenting itself under the name of the Government is immediately overturned by the people, precisely because it does not fulfil the rather contradictory conditions of the programme.

I will venture to say that I fear we are, in this respect, the dupes of one of the strangest illusions which have ever taken possession of the human mind.

Man recoils from trouble--from suffering; and yet he is condemned by nature to the suffering of privation, if he does not take the trouble to work. He has to choose, then, between these two evils. What means can he adopt to avoid both? There remains now, and there will remain, only one way, which is, to enjoy the labour of others. Such a course of conduct prevents the trouble and the satisfaction from preserving their natural proportion, and causes all the trouble to become the lot of one set of persons, and all the satisfaction that of another. This is the origin of slavery and of plunder, whatever its form may be--whether that of wars, impositions, violence, restrictions, frauds, &c.--monstrous abuses, but consistent with the thought which has given them birth. Oppression should be detested and resisted--it can hardly be called absurd.

Slavery is subsiding, thank heaven! and on the other hand, our disposition to defend our property prevents direct and open plunder from being easy.

One thing, however, remains--it is the original inclination which exists in all men to divide the lot of life into two parts, throwing the trouble upon others, and keeping the satisfaction for themselves. It remains to be shown under what new form this sad tendency is manifesting itself.

The oppressor no longer acts directly and with his own powers upon his victim. No, our conscience has become too sensitive for that. The tyrant and his victim are still present, but there is an intermediate person between them, which is the Government--that is, the Law itself. What can be better calculated to silence our scruples, and, which is perhaps better appreciated, to overcome all resistance? We all, therefore, put in our claim, under some pretext or other, and apply to Government. We say to it, "I am dissatisfied at the proportion between my labour and my enjoyments. I should like, for the sake of restoring the desired equilibrium, to take a part of the possessions of others. But this would be dangerous. Could not you facilitate the thing for me? Could you not find me a good place? or check the industry of my competitors? or, perhaps, lend me gratuitously some capital, which you may take from its possessor? Could you not bring up my children at the public expense? or grant me some prizes? or secure me a competence when I have attained my fiftieth year? By this means I shall gain my end with an easy conscience, for the law will have acted for me, and I shall have all the advantages of plunder, without its risk or its disgrace!"

As it is certain, on the one hand, that we are all making some similar request to the Government; and as, on the other, it is proved that Government cannot satisfy one party without adding to the labour of the others, until I can obtain another definition of the word Government, I feel authorised to give my own. Who knows but it may obtain the prize? Here it is:

Government is the great fiction, through which everybody endeavours to live at the expense of everybody else.

For now, as formerly, every one is, more or less, for profiting by the labours of others. No one would dare to profess such a sentiment; he even hides it from himself; and then what is done? A medium is thought of; Government is applied to, and every class in its turn comes to it, and says, "You, who can take justifiably and honestly, take from the public, and we will partake." Alas! Government is only too much disposed to follow this diabolical advice, for it is composed of ministers and officials--of men, in short, who, like all other men, desire in their hearts, and always seize every opportunity with eagerness, to increase their wealth and influence. Government is not slow to perceive the advantages it may derive from the part which is entrusted to it by the public. It is glad to be the judge and the master of the destinies of all; it will take much, for then a large share will remain for itself; it will multiply the number of its agents; it will enlarge the circle of its privileges; it will end by appropriating a ruinous proportion.

But the most remarkable part of it is the astonishing blindness of the public through it all. When successful soldiers used to reduce the vanquished to slavery, they were barbarous, but they were not absurd. Their object, like ours, was to live at other people's expense, and they did not fail to do so. What are we to think of a people who never seem to suspect that reciprocal plunder is no less plunder because it is reciprocal; that it is no less criminal because it is executed legally and with order; that it adds nothing to the public good; that it diminishes it, just in proportion to the cost of the expensive medium which we call the Government?

And it is this great chimera which we have placed, for the edification of the people, as a frontispiece to the Constitution. The following is the beginning of the introductory discourse:--

"France has constituted itself a republic for the purpose of raising all the citizens to an ever-increasing degree of morality, enlightenment, and well-being."

Thus it is France, or an abstraction, which is to raise the French, or realities, to morality, well-being, &c. Is it not by yielding to this strange delusion that we are led to expect everything from an energy not our own? Is it not giving out that there is, independently of the French, a virtuous, enlightened, and rich being, who can and will bestow upon them its benefits? Is not this supposing, and certainly very gratuitously, that there are between France and the French--between the simple, abridged, and abstract denomination of all the individualities, and these individualities themselves--relations as of father to son, tutor to his pupil, professor to his scholar? I know it is often said, metaphorically, "the country is a tender mother." But to show the inanity of the constitutional proposition, it is only needed to show that it may be reversed, not only without inconvenience, but even with advantage. Would it be less exact to say--

"The French have constituted themselves a Republic, to raise France to an ever-increasing degree of morality, enlightenment, and well-being."

Now, where is the value of an axiom where the subject and the attribute may change places without inconvenience? Everybody understands what is meant by this--"The mother will feed the child." But it would be ridiculous to say--"The child will feed the mother."

The Americans formed another idea of the relations of the citizens with the Government when they placed these simple words at the head of their Constitution:--

"We, the people of the United States, for the purpose of forming a more perfect union, of establishing justice, of securing interior tranquillity, of providing for our common defence, of increasing the general well-being, and of securing the benefits of liberty to ourselves and to our posterity, decree," &c.

Here there is no chimerical creation, no abstraction, from which the citizens may demand everything. They expect nothing except from themselves and their own energy.

If I may be permitted to criticise the first words of our Constitution, I would remark, that what I complain of is something more than a mere metaphysical subtilty, as might seem at first sight.

I contend that this personification of Government has been, in past times, and will be hereafter, a fertile source of calamities and revolutions.

There is the public on one side, Government on the other, considered as two distinct beings; the latter bound to bestow upon the former, and the former having the right to claim from the latter, all imaginable human benefits. What will be the consequence?

In fact, Government is not maimed, and cannot be so. It has two hands-- one to receive and the other to give; in other words, it has a rough hand and a smooth one. The activity of the second is necessarily subordinate to the activity of the first. Strictly, Government may take and not restore. This is evident, and may be explained by the porous and absorbing nature of its hands, which always retain a part, and sometimes the whole, of what they touch. But the thing that never was seen, and never will be seen or conceived, is, that Government can restore more to the public than it has taken from it. It is therefore ridiculous for us to appear before it in the humble attitude of beggars. It is radically impossible for it to confer a particular benefit upon any one of the individualities which constitute the community, without inflicting a greater injury upon the community as a whole.

Our requisitions, therefore, place it in a dilemma.

If it refuses to grant the requests made to it, it is accused of weakness, ill-will, and incapacity. If it endeavours to grant them, it is obliged to load the people with fresh taxes--to do more harm than good, and to bring upon itself from another quarter the general displeasure.

Thus, the public has two hopes, and Government makes two promises--many benefits and no taxes. Hopes and promises, which, being contradictory, can never be realised.

Now, is not this the cause of all our revolutions? For, between the Government, which lavishes promises which it is impossible to perform, and the public, which has conceived hopes which can never be realised, two classes of men interpose--the ambitious and the Utopians. It is circumstances which give these their cue. It is enough if these vassals of popularity cry out to the people--"The authorities are deceiving you; if we were in their place, we would load you with benefits and exempt you from taxes."

And the people believe, and the people hope, and the people make a revolution!

No sooner are their friends at the head of affairs, than they are called upon to redeem their pledge. "Give us work, bread, assistance, credit, instruction, colonies," say the people; "and withal deliver us, as you promised, from the talons of the exchequer."

The new Government is no less embarrassed than the former one, for it soon finds that it is much more easy to promise than to perform. It tries to gain time, for this is necessary for maturing its vast projects. At first, it makes a few timid attempts: on one hand it institutes a little elementary instruction; on the other, it makes a little reduction in the liquor tax (1850). But the contradiction is for ever starting up before it; if it would be philanthropic, it must attend to its exchequer; if it neglects its exchequer, it must abstain from being philanthropic.

These two promises are for ever clashing with each other; it cannot be otherwise. To live upon credit, which is the same as exhausting the future, is certainly a present means of reconciling them: an attempt is made to do a little good now, at the expense of a great deal of harm in future. But such proceedings call forth the spectre of bankruptcy, which puts an end to credit. What is to be done then? Why, then, the new Government takes a bold step; it unites all its forces in order to maintain itself; it smothers opinion, has recourse to arbitrary measures, ridicules its former maxims, declares that it is impossible to conduct the administration except at the risk of being unpopular; in short, it proclaims itself governmental. And it is here that other candidates for popularity are waiting for it. They exhibit the same illusion, pass by the same way, obtain the same success, and are soon swallowed up in the same gulf.

We had arrived at this point in February.5 At this time, the illusion which is the subject of this article had made more way than at any former period in the ideas of the people, in connexion with Socialist doctrines. They expected, more firmly than ever, thatGovernment, under a republican form, would open in grand style the source of benefits and close that of taxation. "We have often been deceived," said the people; "but we will see to it ourselves this time, and take care not to be deceived again?"

What could the Provisional Government do? Alas! just that which always is done in similar circumstances--make promises, and gain time. It did so, of course; and to give its promises more weight, it announced them publicly thus:--"Increase of prosperity, diminution of labour, assistance, credit, gratuitous instruction, agricultural colonies, cultivation of waste land, and, at the same time, reduction of the tax on salt, liquor, letters, meat; all this shall be granted when the National Assembly meets."

The National Assembly meets, and, as it is impossible to realise two contradictory things, its task, its sad task, is to withdraw, as gently as possible, one after the other, all the decrees of the Provisional Government. However, in order somewhat to mitigate the cruelty of the deception, it is found necessary to negotiate a little. Certain engagements are fulfilled, others are, in a measure, begun, and therefore the new administration is compelled to contrive some new taxes.

Now, I transport myself, in thought, to a period a few months hence, and ask myself, with sorrowful forebodings, what will come to pass when the agents of the new Government go into the country to collect new taxes upon legacies, revenues, and the profits of agricultural traffic? It is to be hoped that my presentiments may not be verified, but I foresee a difficult part for the candidates for popularity to play.

Read the last manifesto of the Montagnards--that which they issued on the occasion of the election of the President. It is rather long, but at length it concludes with these words:--"Government ought to give a great deal to the people, and take little from them." It is always the same tactics, or, rather, the same mistake.

"Government is bound to give gratuitous instruction and education to all the citizens."

It is bound to give "A general and appropriate professional education, as much as possible adapted to the wants, the callings, and the capacities of each citizen."

It is bound "To teach every citizen his duty to God, to man, and to himself; to develop his sentiments, his tendencies, and his faculties; to teach him, in short, the scientific part of his labour; to make him understand his own interests, and to give him a knowledge of his rights."

It is bound "To place within the reach of all, literature and the arts, the patrimony of thought, the treasures of the mind, and all those intellectual enjoyments which elevate and strengthen the soul."

It is bound "To give compensation for every accident, from fire, inundation, &c., experienced by a citizen." (The et cætera means more than it says.)

It is bound "To attend to the relations of capital with labour, and to become the regulator of credit."

It is bound "To afford important encouragement and efficient protection to agriculture."

It is bound "To purchase railroads, canals, and mines; and, doubtless, to transact affairs with that industrial capacity which characterises it."

It is bound "To encourage useful experiments, to promote and assist them by every means likely to make them successful. As a regulator of credit, it will exercise such extensive influence over industrial and agricultural associations, as shall ensure them success."

Government is bound to do all this, in addition to the services to which it is already pledged; and further, it is always to maintain a menacing attitude towards foreigners; for, according to those who sign the programme, "Bound together by this holy union, and by the precedents of the French Republic, we carry our wishes and hopes beyond the boundaries which despotism has placed between nations. The rights which we desire for ourselves, we desire for all those who are oppressed by the yoke of tyranny; we desire that our glorious army should still, if necessary, be the army of liberty."

You see that the gentle hand of Government--that good hand which gives and distributes, will be very busy under the government of the Montagnards. You think, perhaps, that it will be the same with the rough hand--that hand which dives into our pockets. Do not deceive yourselves. The aspirants after popularity would not know their trade, if they had not the art, when they show the gentle hand, to conceal the rough one. Their reign will assuredly be the jubilee of the tax-payers.

"It is superfluities, not necessaries," they say "which ought to be taxed."

Truly, it will be a good time when the exchequer, for the sake of loading us with benefits, will content itself with curtailing our superfluities!

This is not all. The Montagnards intend that "taxation shall lose its oppressive character, and be only an act of fraternity." Good heavens! I know it is the fashion to thrust fraternity in everywhere, but I did not imagine it would ever be put into the hands of the tax-gatherer.

To come to the details:--Those who sign the programme say, "We desire the immediate abolition of those taxes which affect the absolute necessaries of life, as salt, liquors, &c., &c.

"The reform of the tax on landed property, customs, and patents.

"Gratuitous justice--that is, the simplification of its forms, and reduction of its expenses," (This, no doubt, has reference to stamps.)

Thus, the tax on landed property, customs, patents, stamps, salt, liquors, postage, all are included. These gentlemen have found out the secret of giving an excessive activity to the gentle hand of Government, while they entirely paralyse its rough hand.

Well, I ask the impartial reader, is it not childishness, and more than that, dangerous childishness? Is it not inevitable that we shall have revolution after revolution, if there is a determination never to stop till this contradiction is realised:--"To give nothing to Government and to receive much from it?"

If the Montagnards were to come into power, would they not become the victims of the means which they employed to take possession of it?

Citizens! In all times, two political systems have been in existence, and each may be maintained by good reasons. According to one of them, Government ought to do much, but then it ought to take much. According to the other, this twofold activity ought to be little felt. We have to choose between these two systems. But as regards the third system, which partakes of both the others, and which consists in exacting everything from Government, without giving it anything, it is chimerical, absurd, childish, contradictory, and dangerous. Those who parade it, for the sake of the pleasure of accusing all Governments of weakness, and thus exposing them to your attacks, are only flattering and deceiving you, while they are deceiving themselves.

For ourselves, we consider that Government is and ought to be nothing whatever but common force organized, not to be an instrument of oppression and mutual plunder among citizens; but, on the contrary, to secure to every one his own, and to cause justice and security to reign.

WHAT IS MONEY?

"Hateful money! hateful money!" cried F----, the economist, despairingly, as he came from the Committee of Finance, where a project of paper money had just been discussed.

"What's the matter?" said I. "What is the meaning of this sudden dislike to the most extolled of all the divinities of this world?"

F. Hateful money! hateful money!

B. You alarm me. I hear peace, liberty, and life cried down, and Brutus went so far even as to say, "Virtue! thou art but a name!" But what can have happened?

F. Hateful money! hateful money!

B. Come, come, exercise a little philosophy. What has happened to you? Has Crœsus been affecting you? Has Mondor been playing you false? or has Zoilus been libelling you in the papers?

F. I have nothing to do with Crœsus; my character, by its insignificance, is safe from any slanders of Zoilus; and as to Mondor--

B. Ah! now I have it. How could I be so blind? You, too, are the inventor of a social reorganization--of the F---- system, in fact. Your society is to be more perfect than that of Sparta, and, therefore, all money is to be rigidly banished from it. And the thing that troubles you is, how to persuade your people to empty their purses. What would you have? This is the rock on which all reorganizers split. There is not one, but would do wonders, if he could only contrive to overcome all resisting influences, and if all mankind would consent to become soft wax in his fingers; but men are resolved not to be soft wax; they listen, applaud, or reject, and--go on as before.

F. Thank heaven, I am still free from this fashionable mania. Instead of inventing social laws, I am studying those which it has pleased Providence to invent, and I am delighted to find them admirable in their progressive development. This is why I exclaim, "Hateful money! hateful money!"

B. You are a disciple of Proudhon, then? Well, there is a very simple way for you to satisfy yourself. Throw your purse into the Seine, only reserving a hundred sous, to take an action from the Bank of Exchange.

F. If I cry out against money, is it likely I should tolerate its deceitful substitute?

B. Then I have only one more guess to make. You are a new Diogenes, and are going to victimize me with a discourse á la Seneca, on the contempt of riches.

F. Heaven preserve me from that! For riches, don't you see, are not a little more or a little less money. They are bread for the hungry, clothes for the naked, fuel to warm you, oil to lengthen the day, a career open to your son, a certain portion for your daughter, a day of rest after fatigue, a cordial for the faint, a little assistance slipped into the hand of a poor man, a shelter from the storm, a diversion for a brain worn by thought, the incomparable pleasure of making those happy who are dear to us. Riches are instruction, independence, dignity, confidence, charity; they are progress, and civilization. Riches are the admirable civilizing result of two admirable agents, more civilizing even than riches themselves--labour and exchange.

B. Well! now you seem to be singing the praises of riches, when, a moment ago, you were loading them with imprecations!

F. Why, don't you see that it was only the whim of an economist? I cry out against money, just because everybody confounds it, as you did just now, with riches, and that this confusion is the cause of errors and calamities without number. I cry out against it because its function in society is not understood, and very difficult to explain. I cry out against it, because it jumbles all ideas, causes the means to be taken for the end, the obstacle for the cause, the alpha for the omega; because its presence in the world, though in itself beneficial, has, nevertheless, introduced a fatal notion, a perversion of principles, a contradictory theory, which, in a multitude of forms, has impoverished mankind and deluged the earth with blood. I cry out against it, because I feel that I am incapable of contending against the error to which it has given birth, otherwise than by a long and fastidious dissertation to which no one would listen. Oh! if I could only find a patient and benevolent listener!

B. Well, it shall not be said that for want of a victim you remain in the state of irritation in which you now are. I am listening; speak, lecture, do not restrain yourself in any way.

F. You promise to take an interest?

B. I promise to have patience.

F. That is not much.

B. It is all that I can give. Begin, and explain to me, at first, how a mistake on the subject of cash, if mistake there be, is to be found at the root of all economical errors?

F. Well, now, is it possible that you can conscientiously assure me, that you have never happened to confound wealth with money?

B. I don't know; but, after all, what would be the consequence of such a confusion?

F. Nothing very important. An error in your brain, which would have no influence over your actions; for you see that, with respect to labour and exchange, although there are as many opinions as there are heads, we all act in the same way.

B. Just as we walk upon the same principle, although we are not agreed upon the theory of equilibrium and gravitation.

F. Precisely. A person who argued himself into the opinion that during the night our heads and feet changed places, might write very fine books upon the subject, but still he would walk about like everybody else.

B. So I think. Nevertheless, he would soon suffer the penalty of being too much of a logician.

F. In the same way, a man would die of hunger, who having decided that money is real wealth, should carry out the idea to the end. That is the reason that this theory is false, for there is no true theory but such as results from facts themselves, as manifested at all times, and in all places.

B. I can understand, that practically, and under the influence of personal interest, the fatal effects of the erroneous action would tend to correct an error. But if that of which you speak has so little influence, why does it disturb you so much?

F. Because, when a man, instead of acting for himself, decides for others, personal interest, that ever watchful and sensible sentinel, is no longer present to cry out, "Stop! the responsibility is misplaced." It is Peter who is deceived, and John suffers; the false system of the legislator necessarily becomes the rule of action of whole populations. And observe the difference. When you have money, and are very hungry, whatever your theory on cash may be, what do you do?

B. I go to a baker's, and buy some bread.

F. You do not hesitate about getting rid of your money?

B. The only use of money is to buy what one wants.

F. And if the baker should happen to be thirsty, what does he do?

B. He goes to the wine merchant's, and buys wine with the money I have given him.

F. What! is he not afraid he shall ruin himself?

B. The real ruin would be to go without eating or drinking.

F. And everybody in the world, if he is free, acts in the same manner?

B. Without a doubt. Would you have them die of hunger for the sake of laying by pence?

F. So far from it, that I consider they act wisely, and I only wish that the theory was nothing but the faithful image of this universal practice. But, suppose now that you were the legislator, the absolute king of a vast empire, where there were no gold mines.

B. No unpleasant fiction.

F. Suppose, again, that you were perfectly convinced of this,--that wealth consists solely and exclusively in cash; to what conclusion would you come?

B. I should conclude that there was no other means for me to enrich my people, or for them to enrich themselves, but to draw away the cash from other nations.

F. That is to say, to impoverish them. The first conclusion, then, to which you would arrive would be this,--a nation can only gain when another loses.

B. This axiom has the authority of Bacon and Montaigne.

F. It is not the less sorrowful for that, for it implies--that progress is impossible. Two nations, no more than two men, cannot prosper side by side.

B. It would seem that such is the result of this principle.

F. And as all men are ambitious to enrich themselves, it follows that all are desirous, according to a law of Providence, of ruining their fellow-creatures.

B. This is not Christianity, but it is political economy.

F. Such a doctrine is detestable. But, to continue, I have made you an absolute king. You must not be satisfied with reasoning, you must act. There is no limit to your power. How would you treat this doctrine,--wealth is money?

B. It would be my endeavour to increase, incessantly, among my people the quantity of cash.

F. But there are no mines in your kingdom. How would you set about it? What would you do?

B. I should do nothing: I should merely forbid, on pain of death, that a single crown should leave the country.

F. And if your people should happen to be hungry as well as rich?

B. Never mind. In the system we are discussing, to allow them to export crowns would be to allow them to impoverish themselves.

F. So that, by your own confession, you would force them to act upon a principle equally opposite to that upon which you would yourself act under similar circumstances. Why so?

B. Just because my own hunger touches me, and the hunger of a nation does not touch legislators.

F. Well, I can tell you that your plan would fail, and that no superintendence would be sufficiently vigilant, when the people were hungry, to prevent the crowns from going out and the corn from coming in.

B. If so, this plan, whether erroneous or not, would effect nothing; it would do neither good nor harm, and therefore requires no further consideration.

F. You forget that you are a legislator. A legislator must not be disheartened at trifles, when he is making experiments on others. The first measure not having succeeded, you ought to take some other means of attaining your end.

B. What end?

F. You must have a bad memory. Why, that of increasing, in the midst of your people, the quantity of cash, which is presumed to be true wealth.

B. Ah! to be sure; I beg your pardon. But then you see, as they say of music, a little is enough; and this may be said, I think, with still more reason, of political economy. I must consider. But really I don't know how to contrive--

F. Ponder it well. First, I would have you observe that your first plan solved the problem only negatively. To prevent the crowns from going out of the country is the way to prevent the wealth from diminishing, but it is not the way to increase it.

B. Ah! now I am beginning to see ... the corn which is allowed to come in ... a bright idea strikes me ... the contrivance is ingenious, the means infallible; I am coming to it now.

F. Now, I, in turn, must ask you--to what?

B. Why, to a means of increasing the quantity of cash.

F. How would you set about it, if you please?

B. Is it not evident that if the heap of money is to be constantly increasing, the first condition is that none must be taken from it?

F. Certainly.

B. And the second, that additions must constantly be made to it?

F.. To be sure.

B. Then the problem will be solved, either negatively or positively, as the Socialists say, if on the one hand I prevent the foreigner from taking from it, and on the other I oblige him to add to it.

F. Better and better.

B. And for this there must be two simple laws made, in which cash will not even be mentioned. By the one, my subjects will be forbidden to buy anything abroad; and by the other, they will be required to sell a great deal.

F. A well-advised plan.

B. Is it new? I must take out a patent for the invention.

F. You need do no such thing; you have been forestalled. But you must take care of one thing.

B. What is that?

F. I have made you an absolute king. I understand that you are going to prevent your subjects from buying foreign productions. It will be enough if you prevent them from entering the country. Thirty or forty thousand custom-house officers will do the business.

B. It would be rather expensive. But what does that signify? The money they receive will not go out of the country.

F. True; and in this system it is the grand point. But to ensure a sale abroad, how would you proceed?

B. I should encourage it by prizes, obtained by means of some good taxes laid upon my people.

F. In this case, the exporters, constrained by competition among themselves, would lower their prices in proportion, and it would be like making a present to the foreigner of the prizes or of the taxes.

B. Still, the money would not go out of the country.

F. Of course. That is understood. But if your system is beneficial, the kings around you will adopt it. They will make similar plans to yours; they will have their custom-house officers, and reject your productions; so that with them, as with you, the heap of money may not be diminished.

B. I shall have an army and force their barriers.

F. They will have an army and force yours.

B. I shall arm vessels, make conquests, acquire colonies, and create consumers for my people, who will be obliged to eat our corn and drink our wine.

F. The other kings will do the same. They will dispute your conquests, your colonies, and your consumers; then on all sides there will be war, and all will be uproar.

B. I shall raise my taxes, and increase my custom-house officers, my army, and my navy.

F. The others will do the same.

B. I shall redouble my exertions.

F. The others will redouble theirs. In the meantime, we have no proof that you would succeed in selling to a great extent.

B. It is but too true. It would be well if the commercial efforts would neutralize each other.

F. And the military efforts also. And, tell me, are not these custom-house officers, soldiers, and vessels, these oppressive taxes, this perpetual struggle towards an impossible result, this permanent state of open or secret war with the whole world, are they not the logical and inevitable consequence of the legislators having adopted an idea, which you admit is acted upon by no man who is his own master, that "wealth is cash; and to increase cash, is to increase wealth?"

B. I grant it. Either the axiom is true, and then the legislator ought to act as I have described, although universal war should be the consequence; or it is false; and in this case men, in destroying each other, only ruin themselves.

F. And, remember, that before you became a king, this same axiom had led you by a logical process to the following maxims:--That which one gains, another loses. The profit of one, is the loss of the other:--which maxims imply an unavoidable antagonism amongst all men.

B. It is only too certain. Whether I am a philosopher or a legislator, whether I reason or act upon the principle that money is wealth, I always arrive at one conclusion, or one result:--universal war. It is well that you pointed out the consequences before beginning a discussion upon it; otherwise, I should never have had the courage to follow you to the end of your economical dissertation, for, to tell you the truth, it is not much to my taste.

F. What do you mean? I was just thinking of it when you heard me grumbling against money! I was lamenting that my countrymen have not the courage to study what it is so important that they should know.

B. And yet the consequences are frightful.

F. The consequences! As yet I have only mentioned one. I might have told you of others still more fatal.

B. Yon make my hair stand on end! What other evils can have been caused to mankind by this confusion between money and wealth?

F. It would take me a long time to enumerate them. This doctrine is one of a very numerous family. The eldest, whose acquaintance we have just made, is called the prohibitive system; the next, the colonial system; the third, hatred of capital; the Benjamin, paper money.

B. What! does paper money proceed from the same error?

F. Yes, directly. When legislators, after having ruined men by war and taxes, persevere in their idea, they say to themselves, "If the people suffer, it is because there is not money enough. We must make some." And as it is not easy to multiply the precious metals, especially when the pretended resources of prohibition have been exhausted, they add, "We will make fictitious money, nothing is more easy, and then every citizen will have his pocket-book full of it, and they will all be rich."

B. In fact, this proceeding is more expeditious than the other, and then it does not lead to foreign war.

F. No, but it leads to civil war.

B. You are a grumbler. Make haste and dive to the bottom of the question. I am quite impatient, for the first time, to know if money (or its sign) is wealth.

F. You will grant that men do not satisfy any of their wants immediately with crown pieces. If they are hungry, they want bread; if naked, clothing; if they are ill, they must have remedies; if they are cold, they want shelter and fuel; if they would learn, they must have books; if they would travel, they must have conveyances--and so on. The riches of a country consist in the abundance and proper distribution of all these things. Hence you may perceive and rejoice at the falseness of this gloomy maxim of Bacon's, "What one people gains, another necessarily loses:" a maxim expressed in a still more discouraging manner by Montaigne, in these words: "The profit of one is the loss of another." When Shem, Ham, and Japhet divided amongst themselves the vast solitudes of this earth, they surely might each of them build, drain, sow, reap, and obtain improved lodging, food and clothing, and better instruction, perfect and enrich themselves--in short, increase their enjoyments, without causing a necessary diminution in the corresponding enjoyments of their brothers. It is the same with two nations.

B. There is no doubt that two nations, the same as two men, unconnected with each other, may, by working more, and working better, prosper at the same time, without injuring each other. It is not this which is denied by the axioms of Montaigne and Bacon. They only mean to say, that in the transactions which take place between two nations or two men, if one gains, the other must lose. And this is self-evident, as exchange adds nothing by itself to the mass of those useful things of which you were speaking; for if, after the exchange, one of the parties is found to have gained something, the other will, of course, be found to have lost something.

F. You have formed a very incomplete, nay a false idea of exchange. If Shem is located upon a plain which is fertile in corn, Japhet upon a slope adapted for growing the vine, Ham upon a rich pasturage,--the distinction of their occupations, far from hurting any of them, might cause all three to prosper more. It must be so, in fact, for the distribution of labour, introduced by exchange, will have the effect of increasing the mass of corn, wine, and meat, which is produced, and which is to be shared. How can it be otherwise, if you allow liberty in these transactions? From the moment that any one of the brothers should perceive that labour in company, as it were, was a permanent loss, compared to solitary labour, he would cease to exchange. Exchange brings with it its claim to our gratitude. The fact of its being accomplished, proves that it is a good thing.

B. But Bacon's axiom is true in the case of gold and silver. If we admit that at a certain moment there exists in the world a given quantity, it is perfectly clear that one purse cannot be filled without another being emptied.

F. And if gold is considered to be riches, the natural conclusion is, that displacements of fortune take place among men, but no general progress. It is just what I said when I began. If, on the contrary, you look upon an abundance of useful things, fit for satisfying our wants and our tastes, as true riches, you will see that simultaneous prosperity is possible. Cash serves only to facilitate the transmission of these useful things from one to another, which may be done equally well with an ounce of rare metal like gold, with a pound of more abundant material as silver, or with a hundred-weight of still more abundant metal, as copper. According to that, if the French had at their disposal as much again of all these useful things, France would be twice as rich, although the quantity of cash remained the same; but it would not be the same if there were double the cash, for in that case the amount of useful things would not increase.

B. The question to be decided is, whether the presence of a greater number of crowns has not the effect, precisely, of augmenting the sum of useful things?

F. What connexion can there be between these two terms? Food, clothing, houses, fuel, all come from nature and from labour, from more or less skilful labour exerted upon a more or less liberal nature.

B. You are forgetting one great force, which is--exchange. If you acknowledge that this is a force, as you have admitted that crowns facilitate it, you must also allow that they have an indirect power of production.

F. But I have added, that a small quantity of rare metal facilitates transactions as much as a large quantity of abundant metal; whence it follows, that a people is not enriched by being forced to give up useful things for the sake of having more money.

B. Thus, it is your opinion that the treasures discovered in California will not increase the wealth of the world?

F. I do not believe that, on the whole, they will add much to the enjoyments, to the real satisfactions of mankind. If the Californian gold merely replaces in the world that which has been lost and destroyed, it may have its use. If it increases the amount of cash, it will depreciate it. The gold diggers will be richer than they would have been without it. But those in whose possession the gold is at the moment of its depreciation, will obtain a smaller gratification for the same amount. I cannot look upon this as an increase, but as a displacement of true riches, as I have defined them.

B. All that is very plausible. But you will not easily convince me that I am not richer (all other things being equal) if I have two crowns, than if I had only one.

F. I do not deny it.

B. And what is true of me is true of my neighbour, and of the neighbour of my neighbour, and so on, from one to another, all over the country. Therefore, if every Frenchman has more crowns, France must be more rich.

F. And here you fall into the common mistake of concluding that what affects one affects all, and thus confusing the individual with the general interest.

B. Why, what can be more conclusive? What is true of one, must be so of all! What are all, but a collection of individuals? You might as well tell me that every Frenchman could suddenly grow an inch taller, without the average height of Frenchmen being increased.

F. Your reasoning is apparently sound, I grant you, and that is why the illusion it conceals is so common. However, let us examine it a little. Ten persons were at play. For greater ease, they had adopted the plan of each taking ten counters, and against these they had placed a hundred francs under a candlestick, so that each counter corresponded to ten francs. After the game the winnings were adjusted, and the players drew from the candlestick as many ten francs as would represent the number of counters. Seeing this, one of them, a great arithmetician perhaps, but an indifferent reasoner, said--"Gentlemen, experience invariably teaches me that, at the end of the game, I find myself a gainer in proportion to the number of my counters. Have you not observed the same with regard to yourselves? Thus, what is true of me must be true of each of you, and what is true of each must be true of all. We should, therefore, all of us gain more, at the end of the game, if we all had more counters. Now, nothing can be easier; we have only to distribute twice the number." This was done; but when the game was finished, and they came to adjust the winnings, it was found that the thousand francs under the candlestick had not been miraculously multiplied, according to the general expectation. They had to be divided accordingly, and the only result obtained (chimerical enough) was this;-- every one had, it is true, his double number of counters, but every counter, instead of corresponding to ten francs, only represented five. Thus it was clearly shown, that what is true of each, is not always true of all.

B. I see; you are supposing a general increase of counters, without a corresponding increase of the sum placed under the candlestick.

F. And you are supposing a general increase of crowns, without a corresponding increase of things, the exchange of which is facilitated by these crowns.

B. Do you compare the crowns to counters?

F. In any other point of view, certainly not; but in the case you place before me, and which I have to argue against, I do. Remark one thing. In order that there be a general increase of crowns in a country, this country must have mines, or its commerce must be such as to give useful things in exchange for cash. Apart from these two circumstances, a universal increase is impossible, the crowns only changing hands; and in this case, although it may be very true that each one, taken individually, is richer in proportion to the number of crowns that he has, we cannot draw the inference which you drew just now, because a crown more in one purse implies necessarily a crown less in some other. It is the same as with your comparison of the middle height. If each of us grew only at the expense of others, it would be very true of each, taken individually, that he would be a taller man if he had the chance, but this would never be true of the whole taken collectively.

B. Be it so: but, in the two suppositions that you have made, the increase is real, and you must allow that I am right.

F. To a certain point, gold and silver have a value. To obtain this, men consent to give useful things which have a value also. When, therefore, there are mines in a country, if that country obtains from them sufficient gold to purchase a useful thing from abroad--a locomotive, for instance--it enriches itself with all the enjoyments which a locomotive can procure, exactly as if the machine had been made at home. The question is, whether it spends more efforts in the former proceeding than in the latter? For if it did not export this gold, it would depreciate, and something worse would happen than what you see in California, for there, at least, the precious metals are used to buy useful things made elsewhere. Nevertheless, there is still a danger that they may starve on heaps of gold. What would it be if the law prohibited exportation? As to the second supposition--that of the gold which we obtain by trade; it is an advantage, or the reverse, according as the country stands more or less in need of it, compared to its wants of the useful things which must be given up in order to obtain it. It is not for the law to judge of this, but for those who are concerned in it; for if the law should start upon this principle, that gold is preferable to useful things, whatever may be their value, and if it should act effectually in this sense, it would tend to make France another California, where there would be a great deal of cash to spend, and nothing to buy. It is the very same system which is represented by Midas.

B. The gold which is imported implies that a useful thing is exported, and in this respect there is a satisfaction withdrawn from the country. But is there not a corresponding benefit? And will not this gold be the source of a number of new satisfactions, by circulating from hand to hand, and inciting to labour and industry, until at length it leaves the country in its turn, and causes the importation of some useful thing?

F. Now you have come to the heart of the question. Is it true that a crown is the principle which causes the production of all the objects whose exchange it facilitates? It is very clear that a piece of five francs is only worth five francs; but we are led to believe that this value has a particular character: that it is not consumed like other things, or that it is exhausted very gradually; that it renews itself, as it were, in each transaction; and that, finally this crown has been worth five francs, as many times as it has accomplished transactions--that it is of itself worth all the things for which it has been successively exchanged; and this is believed, because it is supposed that without this crown these things would never have been produced. It is said, the shoemaker would have sold fewer shoes, consequently he would have bought less of the butcher; the butcher would not have gone so often to the grocer, the grocer to the doctor, the doctor to the lawyer, and so on.

B. No one can dispute that.

F. This is the time, then, to analyse the true function of cash, independently of mines and importations. You have a crown. What does it imply in your hands? It is, as it were, the witness and proof that you have, at some time or other, performed some labour, which, instead of profiting by it, you have bestowed upon society in the person of your client. This crown testifies that you have performed a service for society, and, moreover, it shows the value of it. It bears witness, besides, that you have not yet obtained from society a real equivalent service, to which you have a right. To place you in a condition to exercise this right, at the time and in the manner you please, society, by means of your client, has given you an acknowledgment, a title, a privilege from the republic, a counter, a crown in fact, which only differs from executive titles by bearing its value in itself; and if you are able to read with your mind's eye the inscriptions stamped upon it you will distinctly decipher these words:--"Pay the bearer a service equivalent to what he has rendered to society, the value received being shown, proved, and measured by that which is represented by me." Now, you give up your crown to me. Either my title to it is gratuitous, or it is a claim. If you give it me as payment for a service, the following is the result:--your account with society for real satisfactions is regulated, balanced, and closed. You had rendered it a service for a crown, you now restore the crown for a service; as far as you are concerned, you are clear. As for me, I am just in the position in which you were just now. It is I who am now in advance to society for the service which I have just rendered it in your person. I am become its creditor for the value of the labour which I have performed for you, and which I might devote to myself. It is into my hands, then, that the title of this credit--the proof of this social debt--ought to pass. You cannot say that I am any richer; if I am entitled to receive, it is because I have given. Still less can you say that society is a crown richer, because one of its members has a crown more, and another has one less. For if you let me have this crown gratis, it is certain that I shall be so much the richer, but you will be so much the poorer for it; and the social fortune, taken in a mass, will have undergone no change, because as I have already said, this fortune consists in real services, in effective satisfactions, in useful things. You were a creditor to society, you made me a substitute to your rights, and it signifies little to society, which owes a service, whether it pays the debt to you or to me. This is discharged as soon as the bearer of the claim is paid.

B. But if we all had a great number of crowns we should obtain from society many services. Would not that be very desirable?

F. You forget that in the process which I have described, and which is a picture of the reality, we only obtain services from society because we have bestowed some upon it. Whoever speaks of a service, speaks at the same time of a service received and returned, for these two terms imply each other, so that the one must always be balanced by the other. It is impossible for society to render more services than it receives, and yet this is the chimera which is being pursued by means of the multiplication of coins, of paper money, &c.

B. All that appears very reasonable in theory, but in practice I cannot help thinking, when I see how things go, that if, by some fortunate circumstance, the number of crowns could be multiplied in such a way that each of us could see his little property doubled, we should all be more at our ease; we should all make more purchases, and trade would receive a powerful stimulus.

F. More purchases! and what should we buy? Doubtless, useful articles--things likely to procure for us substantial gratification--such as provisions, stuffs, houses, books, pictures. You should begin, then, by proving that all these things create themselves; you must suppose the Mint melting ingots of gold which have fallen from the moon; or that the Board of Assignats be put in action at the national printing office; for you cannot reasonably think that if the quantity of corn, cloth, ships, hats and shoes remains the same, the share of each of us can be greater, because we each go to market with a greater number of real or fictitious money. Remember the players. In the social order, the useful things are what the workers place under the candlestick, and the crowns which circulate from hand to hand are the counters. If you multiply the francs without multiplying the useful things, the only result will be, that more francs will be required for each exchange, just as the players required more counters for each deposit. You have the proof of this in what passes for gold silver, and copper. Why does the same exchange require more copper than silver, more silver than gold? Is it not because these metals are distributed in the world in different proportions?

What reason have you to suppose that if gold were suddenly to become as abundant as silver, it would not require as much of one as of the other to buy a house?

B. You may be right, but I should prefer your being wrong. In the midst of the sufferings which surround us, so distressing in themselves, and so dangerous in their consequences, I have found some consolation in thinking that there was an easy method of making all the members of the community happy.

F. Even if gold and silver were true riches, it would be no easy matter to increase the amount of them in a country where there are no mines.

B. No, but it is easy to substitute something else. I agree with you that gold and silver can do but little service, except as a mere means of exchange. It is the same with paper money, bank-notes, &c. Then, if we had all of us plenty of the latter, which it is so easy to create, we might all buy a great deal, and should want for nothing. Your cruel theory dissipates hopes, illusions, if you will, whose principle is assuredly very philanthropic.

F. Yes, like all other barren dreams formed to promote universal felicity. The extreme facility of the means which you recommend is quite sufficient to expose its hollowness. Do you believe that if it were merely needful to print bank-notes in order to satisfy all our wants, our tastes and desires, that mankind would have been contented to go on till now, without having recourse to this plan? I agree with you that the discovery is tempting. It would immediately banish from the world, not only plunder, in its diversified and deplorable forms, but even labour itself, except the Board of Assignats. But we have yet to learn how assignats are to purchase houses, which no one would have built; corn, which no one would have raised; stuffs, which no one would have taken the trouble to weave.

B. One thing strikes me in your argument. You say yourself, that if there is no gain, at any rate there is no loss in multiplying the instrument of exchange, as is seen by the instance of the players, who were quits by a very mild deception. Why, then, refuse the philosopher's stone, which would teach us the secret of changing flints into gold, and, in the meantime, into paper money? Are you so blindly wedded to your logic, that you would refuse to try an experiment where there can be no risk? If you are mistaken, you are depriving the nation, as your numerous adversaries believe, of an immense advantage. If the error is on their side, no harm can result, as you yourself say, beyond the failure of a hope. The measure, excellent in their opinion, in yours is negative. Let it be tried, then, since the worst which can happen is not the realization of an evil, but the non-realization of a benefit.

F. In the first place, the failure of a hope is a very great misfortune to any people. It is also very undesirable that the Government should announce the re-imposition of several taxes on the faith of a resource which must infallibly fail. Nevertheless, your remark would deserve some consideration, if, after the issue of paper money and its depreciation, the equilibrium of values should instantly and simultaneously take place, in all things and in every part of the country. The measure would tend, as in my example of the players, to a universal mystification, upon which the best thing we could do would be to look at one another and laugh. But this is not in the course of events. The experiment has been made, and every time a despot has altered the money ...

B. Who says anything about altering the money?

F. Why, to force people to take in payment scraps of paper which have been officially baptized francs, or to force them to receive, as weighing five grains, a piece of silver which weighs only two and a half, but which has been officially named a franc, is the same thing, if not worse; and all the reasoning which can be made in favour of assignats has been made in favour of legal false money. Certainly, looking at it, as you did just now, and as you appear to be doing still, if it is believed that to multiply the instruments of exchange is to multiply the exchanges themselves as well as the things exchanged, it might very reasonably be thought that the most simple means was to double the crowns, and to cause the law to give to the half the name and value of the whole. Well, in both cases, depreciation is inevitable. I think I have told you the cause. I must also inform you, that this depreciation, which, with paper, might go on till it came to nothing, is effected by continually making dupes; and of these, poor people, simple persons, workmen and countrymen are the chief.

B. I see; but stop a little. This dose of Economy is rather too strong for once.

F. Be it so. We are agreed, then, upon this point,--that wealth is the mass of useful things Which we produce by labour; or, still better, the result of all the efforts which we make for the satisfaction of our wants and tastes. These useful things are exchanged for each other, according to the convenience of those to whom they belong. There are two forms in these transactions; one is called barter: in this case, a service is rendered for the sake of receiving an equivalent service immediately. In this form, transactions would be exceedingly limited. In order that they may be multiplied, and accomplished independently of time and space amongst persons unknown to each other, and by infinite fractions, an intermediate agent has been necessary,--this is cash. It gives occasion for exchange, which is nothing else but a complicated bargain. This is what has to be remarked and understood. Exchange decomposes itself into two bargains, into two actors, sale and purchase,--the reunion of which is needed to complete it. You sell a service, and receive a crown--then, with this crown, you buy a service. Then only is the bargain complete; it is not till then that your effort has been followed by a real satisfaction. Evidently you only work to satisfy the wants of others, that others may work to satisfy yours. So long as you have only the crown which has been given you for your work, you are only entitled to claim the work of another person. When you have done so, the economical evolution will be accomplished as far as you are concerned, since you will then only have obtained, by a real satisfaction, the true reward for your trouble. The idea of a bargain implies a service rendered, and a service received. Why should it not be the same with exchange, which is merely a bargain in two parts? And here there are two observations to be made. First,--It is a very unimportant circumstance whether there be much or little cash in the world. If there is much, much is required; if there is little, little is wanted, for each transaction: that is all. The second observation is this:--Because it is seen that cash always reappears in every exchange, it has come to be regarded as the sign and the measure of the things exchanged.

B. Will you still deny that cash is the sign of the useful things of which you speak?

F. A louis[6] is no more the sign of a sack of corn, than a sack of corn is the sign of a louis.

B. What harm is there in looking at cash as the sign of wealth?

F. The inconvenience is this,--it leads to the idea that we have only to increase the sign, in order to increase the things signified; and we are in danger of adopting all the false measures which you took when I made you an absolute king. We should go still further. Just as in money we see the sign of wealth, we see also in paper money the sign of money; and thence conclude that there is a very easy and simple method of procuring for everybody the pleasures of fortune.

B. But you will not go so far as to dispute that cash is the measure of values?

F. Yes, certainly, I do go as far as that, for that is precisely where the illusion lies. It has become customary to refer the value of everything to that of cash. It is said, this is worth five, ten, or twenty francs, as we say this weighs five, ten, or twenty grains; this measures five, ten, or twenty yards; this ground contains five, ten, or twenty acres; and hence it has been concluded, that cash is the measure of values.

B. Well, it appears as if it was so.

F. Yes, it appears so, and it is this I complain of, and not of the reality. A measure of length, size, surface, is a quantity agreed upon, and unchangeable. It is not so with the value of gold and silver. This varies as much as that of corn, wine, cloth, or labour, and from the same causes, for it has the same source and obeys the same laws. Gold is brought within our reach, just like iron, by the labour of miners, the advances of capitalists, and the combination of merchants and seamen. It costs more or less, according to the expense of its production, according to whether there is much or little in the market, and whether it is much or little in request; in a word, it undergoes the fluctuations of all other human productions. But one circumstance is singular, and gives rise to many mistakes. When the value of cash varies, the variation is attributed by language to the other productions for which it is exchanged. Thus, let us suppose that all the circumstances relative to gold remain the same, and that the corn harvest has failed. The price of corn will rise. It will be said, "The quarter of corn, which was worth twenty francs, is now worth thirty;" and this will be correct, for it is the value of the corn which has varied, and language agrees with the fact. But let us reverse the supposition: let us suppose that all the circumstances relative to corn remain the same, and that half of all the gold in existence is swallowed up; this time it is the price of gold which will rise. It would seem that we ought to say,--"This Napoleon, which was worth twenty francs, is now worthforty." Now, do you know how this is expressed? Just as if it was the other objects of comparison which had fallen in price, it is said,--"Corn, which was worth twenty francs, is now only worth ten."

B. It all comes to the same thing in the end.

F. No doubt; but only think what disturbances, what cheatings are produced in exchanges, when the value of the medium varies, without our becoming aware of it by a change in the name. Old pieces are issued, or notes bearing the name of twenty francs, and which will bear that name through every subsequent depreciation. The value will be reduced a quarter, a half, but they will still be called pieces or notes of twenty francs. Clever persons will take care not to part with their goods unless for a larger number of notes--in other words, they will ask forty francs for what they would formerly have sold for twenty; but simple persons will be taken in. Many years must pass before all the values will find their proper level. Under the influence of ignorance and custom, the day's pay of a country labourer will remain for a long time at a franc, while the saleable price of all the articles of consumption around him will be rising. He will sink into destitution without being able to discover the cause. In short, since you wish me to finish, I must beg you, before we separate, to fix your whole attention upon this essential point:--When once false money (under whatever form it may take) is put into circulation, depreciation will ensue, and manifest itself by the universal rise of every thing which is capable of being sold. But this rise in prices is not instantaneous and equal for all things. Sharp men, brokers, and men of business, will not suffer by it; for it is their trade to watch the fluctuations of prices, to observe the cause, and even to speculate upon it. But little tradesmen, countrymen, and workmen, will bear the whole weight of it. The rich man is not any the richer for it, but the poor man becomes poorer by it. Therefore, expedients of this kind have the effect of increasing the distance which separates wealth from poverty, of paralysing the social tendencies which are incessantly bringing men to the same level, and it will require centuries for the suffering classes to regain the ground which they have lost in their advance towards equality of condition.

B. Good morning; I shall go and meditate upon the lecture you have been giving me.

F. Have you finished your own dissertation? As for me, I have scarcely begun mine. I have not yet spoken of the hatred of capital, of gratuitous credit--a fatal notion, a deplorable mistake, which takes its rise from the same source.

B. What! does this frightful commotion of the populace against capitalists arise from money being confounded with wealth?

F. It is the result of different causes. Unfortunately, certain capitalists have arrogated to themselves monopolies and privileges which are quite sufficient to account for this feeling. But when the theorists of democracy have wished to justify it, to systematize it, to give it the appearance of a reasonable opinion, and to turn it against the very nature of capital, they have had recourse to that false political economy at whose root the same confusion is always to be found. They have said to the people:--"Take a crown, put it under a glass; forget it for a year; then go and look at it, and you will be convinced that it has not produced ten sous, nor five sous, nor any fraction of a sou. Therefore, money produces no interest." Then, substituting for the word money its pretended sign, capital, they have made it by their logic undergo this modification--"Then capital produces no interest." Then follow this series of consequences--"Therefore he who lends a capital ought to obtain nothing from it; therefore he who lends you a capital, if he gains something by it, is robbing you; therefore all capitalists are robbers; therefore wealth, which ought to serve gratuitously those who borrow it, belongs in reality to those to whom it does not belong; therefore there is no such thing as property; therefore everything belongs to everybody; therefore ..."

B. This is very serious; the more so, from the syllogism being so admirably formed. I should very much like to be enlightened on the subject. But, alas! I can no longer command my attention. There is such a confusion in my head of the words cash, money, services, capital, interest, that, really, I hardly know where I am. We will, if you please, resume the conversation another day.

F. In the meantime, here is a little work entitled Capital and Rent. It may perhaps remove some of your doubts. Just look at it, when you are in want of a little amusement.

B. To amuse me?

F. Who knows? One nail drives in another; one wearisome thing drives away another.

B. I have not yet made up my mind that your views upon cash and political economy in general are correct. But, from your conversation, this is what I have gathered:--That these questions are of the highest importance; for peace or war, order or anarchy, the union or the antagonism of citizens, are at the root of the answer to them. How is it that, in France, a science which concerns us all so nearly, and the diffusion of which would have so decisive an influence upon the fate of mankind, is so little known? Is it that the State does not teach it sufficiently?

F. Not exactly. For, without knowing it, it applies itself to loading everybody's brain with prejudices, and everybody's heart with sentiments favourable to the spirit of anarchy, war, and hatred; so that, when a doctrine of order, peace, and union presents itself, it is in vain that it has clearness and truth on its side,--it cannot gain admittance.

B. Decidedly, you are a frightful grumbler. What interest can the State have in mystifying people's intellects in favour of revolutions, and civil and foreign wars? There must certainly be a great deal of exaggeration in what you say.

F. Consider. At the period when our intellectual faculties begin to develop themselves, at the age when impressions are liveliest, when habits of mind are formed with the greatest ease--when we might look at society and understand it--in a word, as soon as we are seven or eight years old, what does the State do? It puts a bandage over our eyes, takes us gently from the midst of the social circle which surrounds us, to plunge us, with our susceptible faculties, our impressible hearts, into the midst of Roman society. It keeps us there for ten years at least, long enough to make an ineffaceable impression on the brain. Now observe, that Roman society is directly opposed to what our society ought to be. There they lived upon war; here we ought to hate war. There they hated labour; here we ought to live upon labour. There the means of subsistence were founded upon slavery and plunder; here they should be drawn from free industry. Roman society was organised in consequence of its principle. It necessarily admired what made it prosper. There they considered as virtue, what we look upon as vice. Its poets and historians had to exalt what we ought to despise. The very words, liberty, order, justice, people, honour, influence, &c., could not have the same signification at Rome, as they have, or ought to have, at Paris. How can you expect that all these youths who have been at university or conventual schools, with Livy and Quintus Curtius for their catechism, will not understand liberty like the Gracchi, virtue like Cato, patriotism like Cæsar? How can you expect them not to be factious and warlike? How can you expect them to take the slightest interest in the mechanism of our social order? Do you think that their minds have been prepared to understand it? Do you not see that, in order to do so, they must get rid of their present impressions, and receive others entirely opposed to them?

B. What do you conclude from that?

F. I will tell you. The most urgent necessity is, not that the State should teach, but that it should allow education. All monopolies are detestable, but the worst of all is the monopoly of education.

THE LAW.

The law perverted! The law--and, in its wake, all the collective forces of the nation--the law, I say, not only diverted from its proper direction, but made to pursue one entirely contrary! The law become the tool of every kind of avarice, instead of being its check! The law guilty of that very iniquity which it was its mission to punish! Truly, this is a serious fact, if it exists, and one to which I feel bound to call the attention of my fellow-citizens.

We hold from God the gift which, as far as we are concerned, contains all others, Life--physical, intellectual, and moral life.

But life cannot support itself. He who has bestowed it, has entrusted us with the care of supporting it, of developing it, and of perfecting it. To that end, He has provided us with a collection of wonderful faculties; He has plunged us into the midst of a variety of elements. It is by the application of our faculties to these elements, that the phenomena of assimilation and of appropriation, by which life pursues the circle which has been assigned to it, are realized.

Existence, faculties, assimilation--in other words, personality, liberty, property--this is man. It is of these three things that it may be said, apart from all demagogue subtlety, that they are anterior and superior to all human legislation.

It is not because men have made laws, that personality, liberty, and property exist. On the contrary, it is because personality, liberty, and property exist beforehand, that men make laws.

What, then, is law? As I have said elsewhere, it is the collective organization of the individual right to lawful defence.

Nature, or rather God, has bestowed upon every one of us the right to defend his person, his liberty, and his property, since these are the three constituent or preserving elements of life; elements, each of which is rendered complete by the others, and cannot be understood without them. For what are our faculties, but the extension of our personality? and what is property, but an extension of our faculties?

If every man has the right of defending, even by force, his person, his liberty, and his property, a number of men have the right to combine together, to extend, to organize a common force, to provide regularly for this defence.

Collective right, then, has its principle, its reason for existing, its lawfulness, in individual right; and the common force cannot rationally have any other end, or any other mission, than that of the isolated forces for which it is substituted. Thus, as the force of an individual cannot lawfully touch the person, the liberty, or the property of another individual--for the same reason, the common force cannot lawfully be used to destroy the person, the liberty, or the property of individuals or of classes.

For this perversion of force would be, in one case as in the other, in contradiction to our premises. For who will dare to say that force has been given to us, not to defend our rights, but to annihilate the equal rights of our brethren? And if this be not true of every individual force, acting independently, how can it be true of the collective force, which is only the organized union of isolated forces?

Nothing, therefore, can be more evident than this:--The law is the organization of the natural right of lawful defence; it is the substitution of collective for individual forces, for the purpose of acting in the sphere in which they have a right to act, of doing what they have a right to do, to secure persons, liberties, and properties, and to maintain each in its right, so as to cause justice to reign over all.

And if a people established upon this basis were to exist, it seems to me that order would prevail among them in their acts as well as in their ideas. It seems to me that such a people would have the most simple, the most economical, the least oppressive, the least to be felt, the least responsible, the most just, and, consequently, the most solid Government which could be imagined, whatever its political form might be.

For, under such an administration, every one would feel that he possessed all the fulness, as well as all the responsibility of his existence. So long as personal safety was ensured, so long as labour was free, and the fruits of labour secured against all unjust attacks, no one would have any difficulties to contend with in the State. When prosperous, we should not, it is true, have to thank the State for our success; but when unfortunate, we should no more think of taxing it with our disasters, than our peasants think of attributing to it the arrival of hail or of frost. We should know it only by the inestimable blessing of Safety.

It may further be affirmed, that, thanks to the non-intervention of the State in private affairs, our wants and their satisfactions would develop themselves in their natural order. We should not see poor families seeking for literary instruction before they were supplied with bread. We should not see towns peopled at the expense of rural districts, nor rural districts at the expense of towns. We should not see those great displacements of capital, of labour, and of population, which legislative measures occasion; displacements, which render so uncertain and precarious the very sources of existence, and thus aggravate to such an extent the responsibility of Governments.

Unhappily, law is by no means confined to its own department. Nor is it merely in some indifferent and debateable views that it has left its proper sphere. It has done more than this. It has acted in direct opposition to its proper end; it has destroyed its own object; it has been employed in annihilating that justice which it ought to have established, in effacing amongst Rights, that limit which was its true mission to respect; it has placed the collective force in the service of those who wish to traffic, without risk, and without scruple, in the persons, the liberty, and the property of others; it has converted plunder into a right, that it may protect it, and lawful defence into a crime, that it may punish it.

How has this perversion of law been accomplished? And what has resulted from it?

The law has been perverted through the influence of two very different causes--bare egotism and false philanthropy.

Let us speak of the former.

Self-preservation and development is the common aspiration of all men, in such a way that if every one enjoyed the free exercise of his faculties and the free disposition of their fruits, social progress would be incessant, uninterrupted, inevitable.

But there is also another disposition which is common to them. This is, to live and to develop, when they can, at the expense of one another. This is no rash imputation, emanating from a gloomy, uncharitable spirit. History bears witness to the truth of it, by the incessant wars, the migrations of races, sacerdotal oppressions, the universality of slavery, the frauds in trade, and the monopolies with which its annals abound. This fatal disposition has its origin in the very constitution of man--in that primitive, and universal, and invincible sentiment which urges it towards its well-being, and makes it seek to escape pain.

Man can only derive life and enjoyment from a perpetual search and appropriation; that is, from a perpetual application of his faculties to objects, or from labour. This is the origin of property.

But yet he may live and enjoy, by seizing and appropriating the productions of the faculties of his fellow-men. This is the origin of plunder.

Now, labour being in itself a pain, and man being naturally inclined to avoid pain, it follows, and history proves it, that wherever plunder is less burdensome than labour, it prevails; and neither religion nor morality can, in this case, prevent it from prevailing.

When does plunder cease, then? When it becomes less burdensome and more dangerous than labour. It is very evident that the proper aim of law is to oppose the powerful obstacle of collective force to this fatal tendency; that all its measures should be in favour of property, and against plunder.

But the law is made, generally, by one man, or by one class of men. And as law cannot exist without the sanction and the support of a preponderating force, it must finally place this force in the hands of those who legislate.

This inevitable phenomenon, combined with the fatal tendency which, we have said, exists in the heart of man, explains the almost universal perversion of law. It is easy to conceive that, instead of being a check upon injustice, it becomes its most invincible instrument. It is easy to conceive that, according to the power of the legislator, it destroys for its own profit, and in different degrees, amongst the rest of the community, personal independence by slavery, liberty by oppression, and property by plunder.

It is in the nature of men to rise against the injustice of which they are the victims. When, therefore, plunder is organised by law, for the profit of those who perpetrate it, all the plundered classes tend, either by peaceful or revolutionary means, to enter in some way into the manufacturing of laws. These classes, according to the degree of enlightenment at which they have arrived, may propose to themselves two very different ends, when they thus attempt the attainment of their political rights; either they may wish to put an end to lawful plunder, or they may desire to take part in it.

Woe to the nation where this latter thought prevails amongst the masses, at the moment when they, in their turn, seize upon the legislative power!

Up to that time, lawful plunder has been exercised by the few upon the many, as is the case in countries where the right of legislating is confined to a few hands. But now it has become universal, and the equilibrium is sought in universal plunder. The injustice which society contains, instead of being rooted out of it, is generalised. As soon as the injured classes have recovered their political rights, their first thought is, not to abolish plunder (this would suppose them to possess enlightenment, which they cannot have), but to organise against the other classes, and to their own detriment, a system of reprisals,--as if it was necessary, before the reign of justice arrives, that all should undergo a cruel retribution,--some for their iniquity and some for their ignorance.

It would be impossible, therefore, to introduce into society a greater change and a greater evil than this--the conversion of the law into an instrument of plunder.

What would be the consequences of such a perversion? It would require volumes to describe them all. We must content ourselves with pointing out the most striking.

In the first place, it would efface from everybody's conscience the distinction between justice and injustice.

No society can exist unless the laws are respected to a certain degree, but the safest way to make them respected is to make them respectable. When law and morality are in contradiction to each other, the citizen finds himself in the cruel alternative of either losing his moral sense, or of losing his respect for the law--two evils of equal magnitude, between which it would be difficult to choose.

It is so much in the nature of law to support justice, that in the minds of the masses they are one and the same. There is in all of us a strong disposition to regard what is lawful as legitimate, so much so, that many falsely derive all justice from law. It is sufficient, then, for the law to order and sanction plunder, that it may appear to many consciences just and sacred. Slavery, protection, and monopoly find defenders, not only in those who profit by them, but in those who suffer by them. If you suggest a doubt as to the morality of these institutions, it is said directly--"You are a dangerous innovator, a utopian, a theorist, a despiser of the laws; you would shake the basis upon which society rests."

If you lecture upon morality, or political economy, official bodies will be found to make this request to the Government:--

"That henceforth science be taught not only with sole reference to free exchange (to liberty, property, and justice), as has been the case up to the present time, but also, and especially, with reference to the facts and legislation (contrary to liberty, property, and justice) which regulate French industry.

"That, in public pulpits salaried by the treasury, the professor abstain rigorously from endangering in the slightest degree the respect due to the laws now in force."[7]

So that if a law exists which sanctions slavery or monopoly, oppression or plunder, in any form whatever, it must not even be mentioned--for how can it be mentioned without damaging the respect which it inspires? Still further, morality and political economy must be taught in connexion with this law--that is, under the supposition that it must be just, only because it is law.

Another effect of this deplorable perversion of the law is, that it gives to human passions and to political struggles, and, in general, to politics, properly so called, an exaggerated preponderance.

I could prove this assertion in a thousand ways. But I shall confine myself, by way of illustration, to bringing it to bear upon a subject which has of late occupied everybody's mind--universal suffrage.

Whatever may be thought of it by the adepts of the school of Rousseau, which professes to be very far advanced, but which I consider twenty centuries behind, universal suffrage (taking the word in its strictest sense) is not one of those sacred dogmas with respect to which examination and doubt are crimes.

Serious objections may be made to it.

In the first place, the word universal conceals a gross sophism. There are, in France, 36,000,000 of inhabitants. To make the right of suffrage universal, 36,000,000 of electors should be reckoned. The most extended system reckons only 9,000,000. Three persons out of four, then, are excluded; and more than this, they are excluded by the fourth. Upon what principle is this exclusion founded? Upon the principle of incapacity. Universal suffrage, then, means--universal suffrage of those who are capable. In point of fact, who are the capable? Are age, sex, and judicial condemnations the only conditions to which incapacity is to be attached?

On taking a nearer view of the subject, we may soon perceive the motive which causes the right of suffrage to depend upon the presumption of incapacity; the most extended system differing only in this respect from the most restricted, by the appreciation of those conditions on which this incapacity depends, and which constitutes, not a difference in principle, but in degree.

This motive is, that the elector does not stipulate for himself, but for everybody.

If, as the republicans of the Greek and Roman tone pretend, the right of suffrage had fallen to the lot of every one at his birth, it would be an injustice to adults to prevent women and children from voting. Why are they prevented? Because they are presumed to be incapable. And why is incapacity a motive for exclusion? Because the elector does not reap alone the responsibility of his vote; because every vote engages and affects the community at large; because the community has a right to demand some securities, as regards the acts upon which his well-being and his existence depend.

I know what might be said in answer to this. I know what might be objected. But this is not the place to exhaust a controversy of this kind. What I wish to observe is this, that this same controversy (in common with the greater part of political questions) which agitates, excites, and unsettles the nations, would lose almost all its importance if the law had always been what it ought to be.

In fact, if law were confined to causing all persons, all liberties, and all properties to be respected--if it were merely the organisation of individual right and individual defence--if it were the obstacle, the check, the chastisement opposed to all oppression, to all plunder--is it likely that we should dispute much, as citizens, on the subject of the greater or less universality of suffrage? Is it likely that it would compromise that greatest of advantages, the public peace? Is it likely that the excluded classes would not quietly wait for their turn? Is it likely that the enfranchised classes would be very jealous of their privilege? And is it not clear, that the interest of all being one and the same, some would act without much inconvenience to the others?

But if the fatal principle should come to be introduced, that, under pretence of organisation, regulation, protection, or encouragement, the law may take from one party in order to give to another, help itself to the wealth acquired by all the classes that it may increase that of one class, whether that of the agriculturists, the manufacturers, the shipowners, or artists and comedians; then certainly, in this case, there is no class which may not pretend, and with reason, to place its hand upon the law, which would not demand with fury its right of election and eligibility, and which would overturn society rather than not obtain it. Even beggars and vagabonds will prove to you that they have an incontestable title to it. They will say--"We never buy wine, tobacco, or salt, without paying the tax, and a part of this tax is given by law in perquisites and gratuities to men who are richer than we are. Others make use of the law to create an artificial rise in the price of bread, meat, iron, or cloth. Since everybody traffics in law for his own profit, we should like to do the same. We should like to make it produce the right to assistance, which is the poor man's plunder. To effect this, we ought to be electors and legislators, that we may organise, on a large scale, alms for our own class, as you have organised, on a large scale, protection for yours. Don't tell us that you will take our cause upon yourselves, and throw to us 600,000 francs to keep us quiet, like giving us a bone to pick. We have other claims, and, at any rate, we wish to stipulate for ourselves, as other classes have stipulated for themselves!" How is this argument to be answered? Yes, as long as it is admitted that the law may be diverted from its true mission, that it may violate property instead of securing it, everybody will be wanting to manufacture law, either to defend himself against plunder, or to organise it for his own profit. The political question will always be prejudicial, predominant, and absorbing; in a word, there will be fighting around the door of the Legislative Palace. The struggle will be no less furious within it. To be convinced of this, it is hardly necessary to look at what passes in the Chambers in France and in England; it is enough to know how the question stands.

Is there any need to prove that this odious perversion of law is a perpetual source of hatred and discord,--that it even tends to social disorganisation? Look at the United States. There is no country in the world where the law is kept more within its proper domain--which is, to secure to every one his liberty and his property. Therefore, there is no country in the world where social order appears to rest upon a more solid basis. Nevertheless, even in the United States, there are two questions, and only two, which from the beginning have endangered political order. And what are these two questions? That of slavery and that of tariffs; that is, precisely the only two questions in which, contrary to the general spirit of this republic, law has taken the character of a plunderer. Slavery is a violation, sanctioned by law, of the rights of the person. Protection is a violation perpetrated by the law upon the rights of property; and certainly it is very remarkable that, in the midst of so many other debates, this double legal scourge, the sorrowful inheritance of the Old World, should be the only one which can, and perhaps will, cause the rupture of the Union. Indeed, a more astounding fact, in the heart of society, cannot be conceived than this:--That law should have become an instrument of injustice. And if this fact occasions consequences so formidable to the United States, where there is but one exception, what must it be with us in Europe, where it is a principle--a system?

M. Montalembert, adopting the thought of a famous proclamation of M. Carlier, said, "We must make war against socialism." And by socialism, according to the definition of M. Charles Dupin, he meant plunder.

But what plunder did he mean? For there are two sorts--extra-legal and legal plunder.

As to extra-legal plunder, such as theft, or swindling, which is defined, foreseen, and punished by the penal code, I do not think it can be adorned by the name of socialism. It is not this which systematically threatens the foundations of society. Besides, the war against this kind of plunder has not waited for the signal of M. Montalembert or M. Carlier. It has gone on since the beginning of the world; France was carrying it on long before the revolution of February--long before the appearance of socialism--with all the ceremonies of magistracy, police, gendarmerie, prisons, dungeons, and scaffolds. It is the law itself which is conducting this war, and it is to be wished, in my opinion, that the law should always maintain this attitude with respect to plunder.

But this is not the case. The law sometimes takes its own part. Sometimes it accomplishes it with its own hands, in order to save the parties benefited the shame, the danger, and the scruple. Sometimes it places all this ceremony of magistracy, police, gendarmerie, and prisons, at the service of the plunderer, and treats the plundered party, when he defends himself, as the criminal. In a word, there is a legal plunder, and it is, no doubt, this which is meant by M. Montalembert.

This plunder may be only an exceptional blemish in the legislation of a people, and in this case, the best thing that can be done is, without so many speeches and lamentations, to do away with it as soon as possible, notwithstanding the clamours of interested parties. But how is it to be distinguished? Very easily. See whether the law takes from some persons that which belongs to them, to give to others what does not belong to them. See whether the law performs, for the profit of one citizen, and, to the injury of others, an act which this citizen cannot perform without committing a crime. Abolish this law without delay; it is not merely an iniquity--it is a fertile source of iniquities, for it invites reprisals; and if you do not take care, the exceptional case will extend, multiply, and become systematic. No doubt the party benefited will exclaim loudly; he will assert his acquired rights. He will say that the State is bound to protect and encourage his industry; he will plead that it is a good thing for the State to be enriched, that it may spend the more, and thus shower down salaries upon the poor workmen. Take care not to listen to this sophistry, for it is just by the systematising of these arguments that legal plunder becomes systematised.

And this is what has taken place. The delusion of the day is to enrich all classes at the expense of each other; it is to generalise plunder under pretence of organising it. Now, legal plunder may be exercised in an infinite multitude of ways. Hence come an infinite multitude of plans for organisation; tariffs, protection, perquisites, gratuities, encouragements, progressive taxation, gratuitous instruction, right to labour, right to profit, right to wages, right to assistance, right to instruments of labour, gratuity of credit, &c., &c. And it is all these plans, taken as a whole, with what they have in common, legal, plunder, which takes the name of socialism.

Now socialism, thus defined, and forming a doctrinal body, what other war would you make against it than a war of doctrine? You find this doctrine false, absurd, abominable. Refute it. This will be all the more easy, the more false, the more absurd and the more abominable it is. Above all, if you wish to be strong, begin by rooting out of your legislation every particle of socialism which may have crept into it,--and this will be no light work.

M. Montalembert has been reproached with wishing to turn brute force against socialism. He ought to be exonerated from this reproach, for he has plainly said:--"The war which we must make against socialism must be one which is compatible with the law, honour, and justice."

But how is it that M. Montalembert does not see that he is placing himself in a vicious circle? You would oppose law to socialism. But it is the law which socialism invokes. It aspires to legal, not extra-legal plunder. It is of the law itself, like monopolists of all kinds, that it wants to make an instrument; and when once it has the law on its side, how will you be able to turn the law against it? How will you place it under the power of your tribunals, your gendarmes, and of your prisons? What will you do then? You wish to prevent it from taking any part in the making of laws. You would keep it outside the Legislative Palace. In this you will not succeed, I venture to prophesy, so long as legal plunder is the basis of the legislation within.

It is absolutely necessary that this question of legal plunder should be determined, and there are only three solutions of it:--

1. When the few plunder the many.

2. When everybody plunders everybody else.

3. When nobody plunders anybody.

Partial plunder, universal plunder, absence of plunder, amongst these we have to make our choice. The law can only produce one of these results.

Partial plunder.--This is the system which prevailed so long as the elective privilege was partial--a system which is resorted to to avoid the invasion of socialism.

Universal plunder.--We have been threatened by this system when the elective privilege has become universal; the masses having conceived the idea of making law, on the principle of legislators who had preceded them.

Absence of plunder.--This is the principle of justice, peace, order, stability, conciliation, and of good sense, which I shall proclaim with all the force of my lungs (which is very inadequate, alas!) till the day of my death.

And, in all sincerity, can anything more be required at the hands of the law? Can the law, whose necessary sanction is force, be reasonably employed upon anything beyond securing to every one his right? I defy any one to remove it from this circle without perverting it, and consequently turning force against right. And as this is the most fatal, the most illogical social perversion which can possibly be imagined, it must be admitted that the true solution, so much sought after, of the social problem, is contained in these simple words--LAW IS ORGANISED JUSTICE.

Now it is important to remark, that to organise justice by law, that is to say by force, excludes the idea of organising by law, or by force any manifestation whatever of human activity--labour, charity, agriculture, commerce, industry, instruction, the fine arts, or religion; for any one of these organisations would inevitably destroy the essential organisation. How, in fact, can we imagine force encroaching upon the liberty of citizens without infringing upon justice, and so acting against its proper aim?

Here I am encountering the most popular prejudice of our time. It is not considered enough that law should be just, it must be philanthropic. It is not sufficient that it should guarantee to every citizen the free and inoffensive exercise of his faculties, applied to his physical, intellectual, and moral development; it is required to extend well-being, instruction, and morality, directly over the nation. This is the fascinating side of socialism.

But, I repeat it, these two missions of the law contradict each other. We have to choose between them. A citizen cannot at the same time be free and not free. M. de Lamartine wrote to me one day thus:--"Your doctrine is only the half of my programme; you have stopped at liberty, I go on to fraternity." I answered him:--"The second part of your programme will destroy the first." And in fact it is impossible for me to separate the word fraternity from the word voluntary. I cannot possibly conceive fraternity legally enforced, without liberty being legally destroyed, and justice legally trampled under foot. Legal plunder has two roots: one of them, as we have already seen, is in human egotism; the other is in false philanthropy.

Before I proceed, I think I ought to explain myself upon the word plunder.8

I do not take it, as it often is taken, in a vague, undefined, relative, or metaphorical sense. I use it in its scientific acceptation, and as expressing the opposite idea to property. When a portion of wealth passes out of the hands of him who has acquired it, without his consent, and without compensation, to him who has not created it, whether by force or by artifice, I say that property is violated, that plunder is perpetrated. I say that this is exactly what the law ought to repress always and everywhere. If the law itself performs the action it ought to repress, I say that plunder is still perpetrated, and even, in a social point of view, under aggravated circumstances. In this case, however, he who profits from the plunder is not responsible for it; it is the law, the lawgiver, society itself, and this is where the political danger lies.

It is to be regretted that there is something offensive in the word. I have sought in vain for another, for I would not wish at any time, and especially just now, to add an irritating word to our dissensions; therefore, whether I am believed or not, I declare that I do not mean to accuse the intentions nor the morality of anybody. I am attacking an idea which I believe to be false-- a system which appears to me to be unjust; and this is so independent of intentions, that each of us profits by it without wishing it, and suffers from it without being aware of the cause. Any person must write under the influence of party spirit or of fear, who would call in question the sincerity of protectionism, of socialism, and even of communism, which are one and the same plant, in three different periods of its growth. All that can be said is, that plunder is more visible by its partiality in protectionism,9 and by its universality in communism; whence it follows that, of the three systems, socialism is still the most vague, the most undefined, and consequently the most sincere.

Be it as it may, to conclude that legal plunder has one of its roots in false philanthropy, is evidently to put intentions out of the question.

With this understanding, let us examine the value, the origin, and the tendency of this popular aspiration, which pretends to realise the general good by general plunder.

The Socialists say, since the law organises justice, why should it not organise labour, instruction, and religion?

Why? Because it could not organise labour, instruction, and religion, without disorganising justice.

For, remember, that law is force, and that consequently the domain of the law cannot lawfully extend beyond the domain of force.

When law and force keep a man within the bounds of justice, they impose nothing upon him but a mere negation. They only oblige him to abstain from doing harm. They violate neither his personality, his liberty, nor his property. They only guard the personality, the liberty, the property of others. They hold themselves on the defensive; they defend the equal right of all. They fulfil a mission whose harmlessness is evident, whose utility is palpable, and whose legitimacy is not to be disputed. This is so true that, as a friend of mine once remarked to me, to say that the aim of the law is to cause justice to reign, is to use an expression which is not rigorously exact. It ought to be said, the aim of the law is to prevent injustice from reigning. In fact, it is not justice which has an existence of its own, it is injustice. The one results from the absence of the other.

But when the law, through the medium of its necessary agent--force, imposes a form of labour, a method or a subject of instruction, a creed, or a worship, it is no longer negative; it acts positively upon men. It substitutes the will of the legislator for their own will, the initiative of the legislator for their own initiative. They have no need to consult, to compare, or to foresee; the law does all that for them. The intellect is for them a useless lumber; they cease to be men; they lose their personality, their liberty, their property.

Endeavour to imagine a form of labour imposed by force, which is not a violation of liberty; a transmission of wealth imposed by force, which is not a violation of property. If you cannot succeed in reconciling this, you are bound to conclude that the law cannot organise labour and industry without organising injustice.

When, from the seclusion of his cabinet, a politician takes a view of society, he is struck with the spectacle of inequality which presents itself. He mourns over the sufferings which are the lot of so many of our brethren, sufferings whose aspect is rendered yet more sorrowful by the contrast of luxury and wealth.

He ought, perhaps, to ask himself, whether such a social state has not been caused by the plunder of ancient times, exercised in the way of conquests; and by plunder of later times, effected through the medium of the laws? He ought to ask himself whether, granting the aspiration of all men after well-being and perfection, the reign of justice would not suffice to realise the greatest activity of progress, and the greatest amount of equality compatible with that individual responsibility which God has awarded as a just retribution of virtue and vice?

He never gives this a thought. His mind turns towards combinations, arrangements, legal or factitious organisations. He seeks the remedy in perpetuating and exaggerating what has produced the evil.

For, justice apart, which we have seen is only a negation, is there any one of these legal arrangements which does not contain the principle of plunder?

You say, "There are men who have no money," and you apply to the law. But the law is not a self-supplied fountain, whence every stream may obtain supplies independently of society. Nothing can enter the public treasury, in favour of one citizen or one class, but what other citizens and other classes have been forced to send to it. If every one draws from it only the equivalent of what he has contributed to it, your law, it is true, is no plunderer, but it does nothing for men who want money--it does not promote equality. It can only be an instrument of equalisation as far as it takes from one party to give to another, and then it is an instrument of plunder. Examine, in this light, the protection of tariffs, prizes for encouragement, right to profit, right to labour, right to assistance, right to instruction, progressive taxation, gratuitousness of credit, social workshops, and you will always find at the bottom legal plunder, organised injustice.

You say, "There are men who want knowledge," and you apply to the law. But the law is not a torch which sheds light abroad which is peculiar to itself. It extends over a society where there are men who have knowledge, and others who have not; citizens who want to learn, and others who are disposed to teach. It can only do one of two things: either allow a free operation to this kind of transaction, i.e., let this kind of want satisfy itself freely; or else force the will of the people in the matter, and take from some of them sufficient to pay professors commissioned to instruct others gratuitously. But, in this second case, there cannot fail to be a violation of liberty and property,--legal plunder.

You say, "Here are men who are wanting in morality or religion," and you apply to the law; but law is force, and need I say how far it is a violent and absurd enterprise to introduce force in these matters?

As the result of its systems and of its efforts, it would seem that socialism, notwithstanding all its self-complacency, can scarcely help perceiving the monster of legal plunder. But what does it do? It disguises it cleverly from others, and even from itself, under the seductive names of fraternity, solidarity, organisation, association. And because we do not ask so much at the hands of the law, because we only ask it for justice, it supposes that we reject fraternity, solidarity, organisation, and association; and they brand us with the name of individualists.

We can assure them that what we repudiate is, not natural organisation, but forced organisation.

It is not free association, but the forms of association which they would impose upon us.

It is not spontaneous fraternity, but legal fraternity.

It is not providential solidarity, but artificial solidarity, which is only an unjust displacement of responsibility.

Socialism, like the old policy from which it emanates, confounds Government and society. And so, every time we object to a thing being done by Government, it concludes that we object to its being done at all. We disapprove of education by the State--then we are against education altogether. We object to a State religion--then we would have no religion at all. We object to an equality which is brought about by the State--then we are against equality, &c., &c. They might as well accuse us of wishing men not to eat, because we object to the cultivation of corn by the State.

How is it that the strange idea of making the law produce what it does not contain--prosperity, in a positive sense, wealth, science, religion--should ever have gained ground in the political world? The modern politicians, particularly those of the Socialist school, found their different theories upon one common hypothesis; and surely a more strange, a more presumptuous notion, could never have entered a human brain.

They divide mankind into two parts. Men in general, except one, form the first; the politician himself forms the second, which is by far the most important.

In fact, they begin by supposing that men are devoid of any principle of action, and of any means of discernment in themselves; that they have no moving spring in them; that they are inert matter, passive particles, atoms without impulse; at best a vegetation indifferent to its own mode of existence, susceptible of receiving, from an exterior will and hand, an infinite number of forms, more or less symmetrical, artistic, and perfected.

Moreover, every one of these politicians does not scruple to imagine that he himself is, under the names of organiser, discoverer, legislator, institutor or founder, this will and hand, this universal spring, this creative power, whose sublime mission it is to gather together these scattered materials, that is, men, into society.

Starting from these data, as a gardener, according to his caprice, shapes his trees into pyramids, parasols, cubes, cones, vases, espaliers, distaffs, or fans; so the Socialist, following his chimera, shapes poor humanity into groups, series, circles, sub-circles, honeycombs, or social workshops, with all kinds of variations. And as the gardener, to bring his trees into shape, wants hatchets, pruning-hooks, saws, and shears, so the politician, to bring society into shape, wants the forces which he can only find in the laws; the law of customs, the law of taxation, the law of assistance, and the law of instruction.

It is so true, that the Socialists look upon mankind as a subject for social combinations, that if, by chance, they are not quite certain of the success of these combinations, they will request a portion of mankind, as a subject to experiment upon. It is well known how popular the idea of trying all systems is, and one of their chiefs has been known seriously to demand of the Constituent Assembly a parish, with all its inhabitants, upon which to make his experiments.

It is thus that an inventor will make a small machine before he makes one of the regular size. Thus the chemist sacrifices some substances, the agriculturist some seed and a corner of his field, to make trial of an idea.

But, then, think of the immeasurable distance between the gardener and his trees, between the inventor and his machine, between the chemist and his substances, between the agriculturist and his seed! The Socialist thinks, in all sincerity, that there is the same distance between himself and mankind.

It is not to be wondered at that the politicians of the nineteenth century look upon society as an artificial production of the legislator's genius. This idea, the result of a classical education, has taken possession of all the thinkers and great writers of our country.

To all these persons, the relations between mankind and the legislator appear to be the same as those which exist between the clay and the potter.

Moreover, if they have consented to recognise in the heart of man a principle of action, and in his intellect a principle of discernment, they have looked upon this gift of God as a fatal one, and thought that mankind, under these two impulses, tended fatally towards ruin. They have taken it for granted, that if abandoned to their own inclinations, men would only occupy themselves with religion to arrive at atheism, with instruction to come to ignorance, and with labour and exchange to be extinguished in misery.

Happily, according to these writers, there are some men, termed governors and legislators, upon whom Heaven has bestowed opposite tendencies, not for their own sake only, but for the sake of the rest of the world.

Whilst mankind tends to evil, they incline to good; whilst mankind is advancing towards darkness, they are aspiring to enlightenment; whilst mankind is drawn towards vice, they are attracted by virtue. And, this granted, they demand the assistance of force, by means of which they are to substitute their own tendencies for those of the human race.

It is only needful to open, almost at random, a book on philosophy, polities, or history, to see how strongly this idea--the child of classical studies and the mother of socialism--is rooted in our country; that mankind is merely inert matter, receiving life, organisation, morality, and wealth from power; or, rather, and still worse--that mankind itself tends towards degradation, and is only arrested in its tendency by the mysterious hand of the legislator. Classical conventionalism shows us everywhere, behind passive society, a hidden power, under the names of Law, or Legislator (or, by a mode of expression which refers to some person or persons of undisputed weight and authority, but not named), which moves, animates, enriches, and regenerates mankind.

We will give a quotation from Bossuet:--

"One of the things which was the most strongly impressed (by whom?) upon the mind of the Egyptians, was the love of their country.... Nobody was allowed to be useless to the State; the law assigned to every one his employment, which descended from father to son. No one was permitted to have two professions, nor to adopt another.... But there was one occupation which was obliged to be common to all,--this was the study of the laws and of wisdom; ignorance of religion and the political regulations of the country was excused in no condition of life. Moreover, every profession had a district assigned to it (by whom?).... Amongst good laws, one of the best things was, that everybody was taught to observe them (by whom?). Egypt abounded with wonderful inventions, and nothing was neglected which could render life comfortable and tranquil."

Thus men, according to Bossuet, derive nothing from themselves; patriotism, wealth, inventions, husbandry, science--all come to them by the operation of the laws, or by kings. All they have to do is to be passive. It is on this ground that Bossuet takes exception, when Diodorus accuses the Egyptians of rejecting wrestling and music. "How is that possible," says he, "since these arts were invented by Trismegistus?"

It is the same with the Persians:--

"One of the first cares of the prince was to encourage agriculture.... As there were posts established for the regulation of the armies, so there were offices for the superintending of rural works.... The respect with which the Persians were inspired for royal authority was excessive."

The Greeks, although full of mind, were no less strangers to their own responsibilities; so much so, that of themselves, like dogs and horses, they would not have ventured upon the most simple games. In a classical sense, it is an undisputed thing that everything comes to the people from without.

"The Greeks, naturally full of spirit and courage, had been early cultivated by kings and colonies who had come from Egypt. From them they had learned the exercises of the body, foot races, and horse and chariot races.... The best thing that the Egyptians had taught them was to become docile, and to allow themselves to be formed by the laws for the public good."

Fenelon.--Reared in the study and admiration of antiquity, and a witness of the power of Louis XIV., Fenelon naturally adopted the idea that mankind should be passive, and that its misfortunes and its prosperities, its virtues and its vices, are caused by the external influence which is exercised upon it by the law, or by the makers of the law. Thus, in his Utopia of Salentum, he brings the men, with their interests, their faculties, their desires, and their possessions, under the absolute direction of the legislator. Whatever the subject may be, they themselves have no voice in it--the prince judges for them. The nation is just a shapeless mass, of which the prince is the soul. In him resides the thought, the foresight, the principle of all organisation, of all progress; on him, therefore, rests all the responsibility.

In proof of this assertion, I might transcribe the whole of the tenth book of "Telemachus." I refer the reader to it, and shall content myself with quoting some passages taken at random from this celebrated work, to which, in every other respect, I am the first to render justice.

With the astonishing credulity which characterizes the classics, Fenelon, against the authority of reason and of facts, admits the general felicity of the Egyptians, and attributes it, not to their own wisdom, but to that of their kings:--

"We could not turn our eyes to the two shores, without perceiving rich towns and country seats, agreeably situated; fields which were covered every year, without intermission, with golden crops; meadows full of flocks; labourers bending under the weight of fruits which the earth lavished on its cultivators; and shepherds who made the echoes around repeat the soft sounds of their pipes and flutes. 'Happy,' said Mentor, 'is that people which is governed by a wise king.'.... Mentor afterwards desired me to remark the happiness and abundance which was spread over all the country of Egypt, where twenty-two thousand cities might be counted. He admired the excellent police regulations of the cities; the justice administered in favour of the poor against the rich; the good education of the children, who were accustomed to obedience, labour, and the love of arts and letters; the exactness with which all the ceremonies of religion were performed; the disinterestedness, the desire of honour, the fidelity to men, and the fear of the gods, with which every father inspired his children. He could not sufficiently admire the prosperous state of the country. 'Happy,' said he, 'is the people whom a wise king rules in such a manner.'"

Fenelon's idyl on Crete is still more fascinating. Mentor is made to say:--

"All that you will see in this wonderful island is the result of the laws of Minos. The education which the children receive renders the body healthy and robust. They are accustomed, from the first, to a frugal and laborious life; it is supposed that all the pleasures of sense enervate the body and the mind; no other pleasure is presented to them but that of being invincible by virtue, that of acquiring much glory.... there they punish three vices which go unpunished amongst other people--ingratitude, dissimulation, and avarice. As to pomp and dissipation, there is no need to punish these, for they are unknown in Crete...... No costly furniture, no magnificent clothing, no delicious feasts, no gilded palaces are allowed."

It is thus that Mentor prepares his scholar to mould and manipulate, doubtless with the most philanthropic intentions, the people of Ithaca, and, to confirm him in these ideas, he gives him the example of Salentum.

It is thus that we receive our first political notions. We are taught to treat men very much as Oliver de Serres teaches farmers to manage and to mix the soil.

Montesquieu.--"To sustain the spirit of commerce, it is necessary that all the laws should favour it; that these same laws, by their regulations in dividing the fortunes in proportion as commerce enlarges them, should place every poor citizen in sufficiently easy circumstances to enable him to work like the others, and every rich citizen in such mediocrity that he must work, in order to retain or to acquire."

Thus the laws are to dispose of all fortunes.

"Although, in a democracy, real equality be the soul of the State, yet it is so difficult to establish, that an extreme exactness in this matter would not always be desirable. It is sufficient that a census be established to reduce or fix the differences to a certain point. After which, it is for particular laws to equalise, as it were, the inequality, by burdens imposed upon the rich, and reliefs granted to the poor."

Here, again, we see the equalisation of fortunes by law, that is, by force.

"There were, in Greece, two kinds of republics. One was military, as Lacedæmon; the other commercial, as Athens. In the one it was wished (by whom?) that the citizens should be idle: in the other, the love of labour was encouraged.

"It is worth our while to pay a little attention to the extent of genius required by these legislators, that we may see how, by confounding all the virtues, they showed their wisdom to the world. Lycurgus, blending theft with the spirit of justice, the hardest slavery with extreme liberty, the most atrocious sentiments with the greatest moderation, gave stability to his city. He seemed to deprive it of all its resources, arts, commerce, money, and walls; there Was ambition without the hope of rising; there were natural sentiments where the individual was neither child, nor husband, nor father. Chastity even was deprived of modesty. By this road Sparta was led on to grandeur and to glory.

"The phenomenon which we observe in the institutions of Greece has been seen in the midst of the degeneracy and corruption of our modern times. An honest legislator has formed a people where probity has appeared as natural as bravery among the Spartans. Mr. Penn is a true Lycurgus, and although the former had peace for his object, and the latter war, they resemble each other in the singular path along which they have led their people, in their influence over free men, in the prejudices which they have overcome, the passions they have subdued.

"Paraguay furnishes us with another example. Society has been accused of the crime of regarding the pleasure of commanding as the only good of life; but it will always be a noble thing to govern men by making them happy.

"Those who desire to form similar institutions, will establish community of property, as in the republic of Plato, the same reverence which he enjoined for the gods, separation from strangers for the preservation of morality, and make the city and not the citizens create commerce: they should give our arts without our luxury, our wants without our desires."

Vulgar infatuation may exclaim, if it likes:--"It is Montesquieu! magnificent! sublime!" I am not afraid to express my opinion, and to say:--"What! you have the face to call that fine? It is frightful! it is abominable! and these extracts, which I might multiply, show that, according to Montesquieu, the persons, the liberties, the property, mankind itself, are nothing but materials to exercise the sagacity of lawgivers."

Rousseau.--Although this politician, the paramount authority of the Democrats, makes the social edifice rest upon the general will, no one has so completely admitted the hypothesis of the entire passiveness of human nature in the presence of the lawgiver:--

"If it is true that a great prince is a rare thing, how much more so must a great lawgiver be? The former has only to follow the pattern proposed to him by the latter. This latter is the mechanician who invents the machine; the former is merely the workman who sets it in motion."

And what part have men to act in all this? That of the machine, which is set in motion; or rather, are they not the brute matter of which the machine is made? Thus, between the legislator and the prince, between the prince and his subjects, there are the same relations as those which exist between the agricultural writer and the agriculturist, the agriculturist and the clod. At what a vast height, then, is the politician placed, who rules over legislators themselves, and teaches them their trade in such imperative terms as the following:--

"Would you give consistency to the State? Bring the extremes together as much as possible. Suffer neither wealthy persons nor beggars.

"If the soil is poor and barren, or the country too much confined for the inhabitants, turn to industry and the arts, whose productions you will exchange for the provisions which you require.... On a good soil, if you are short of inhabitants, give all your attention to agriculture, which multiplies men, and banish the arts, which only serve to depopulate the country.... Pay attention to extensive and convenient coasts. Cover the sea with vessels, and you will have a brilliant and short existence. If your seas wash only inaccessible rocks, let the people be barbarous, and eat fish; they will live more quietly, perhaps better, and, most certainly, more happily. In short, besides those maxims which are common to all, every people has its own particular circumstances, which demand a legislation peculiar to itself.

"It was thus that the Hebrews formerly, and the Arabs more recently, had religion for their principal object; that of the Athenians was literature; that of Carthage and Tyre, commerce; of Rhodes, naval affairs; of Sparta, war; and of Rome, virtue. The author of the 'Spirit of Laws' has shown the art by which the legislator should frame his institutions towards each of these objects.... But if the legislator, mistaking his object, should take up a principle different from that which arises from the nature of things; if one should tend to slavery, and the other to liberty; if one to wealth, and the other to population; one to peace, and the other to conquests; the laws will insensibly become enfeebled, the Constitution will be impaired, and the State will be subject to incessant agitations until it is destroyed, or becomes changed, and invincible Nature regains her empire."

But if Nature is sufficiently invincible to regain its empire, why does not Kousseau admit that it had no need of the legislator to gainits empire from the beginning? Why does he not allow that, by obeying their own impulse, men would, of themselves, apply agriculture to a fertile district, and commerce to extensive and commodious coasts, without the interference of a Lycurgus, a Solon, or a Rousseau, who would undertake it at the risk of deceiving themselves?

Be that as it may, we see with what a terrible responsibility Rousseau invests inventors, institutors, conductors, and manipulators of societies. He is, therefore, very exacting with regard to them.

"He who dares to undertake the institutions of a people, ought to feel that he can, as it were, transform every individual, who is by himself a perfect and solitary whole, receiving his life and being from a larger whole of which he forms a part; he must feel that he can change the constitution of man, to fortify it, and substitute a partial and moral existence for the physical and independent one which we have all received from nature. In a word, he must deprive man of his own powers, to give him others which are foreign to him."

Poor human nature! What would become of its dignity if it were entrusted to the disciples of Rousseau?

Raynal.--"The climate, that is, the air and the soil, is the first element for the legislator. His resources prescribe to him his duties. First, he must consult his local position. A population dwelling upon maritime shores must have laws fitted for navigation.... If the colony is located in an inland region, a legislator must provide for the nature of the soil, and for its degree of fertility....

"It is more especially in the distribution of property that the wisdom of legislation will appear. As a general rule, and in every country, when a new colony is founded, land should be given to each man, sufficient for the support of his family....

"In an uncultivated island, which you are colonizing with children, it will only be needful to let the germs of truth expand in the developments of reason! But when you establish old people in a new country, the skill consists in only allowing it those injurious opinions and customs which it is impossible to cure and correct. If you wish to prevent them from being perpetuated, you will act upon the rising generation by a general and public education of the children. A prince, or legislator, ought never to found a colony without previously sending wise men there to instruct the youth.... In a new colony, every facility is open to the precautions of the legislator who desires to purify the tone and the manners of the people. If he has genius and virtue, the lands and the men which are at his disposal will inspire his soul with a plan of society which a writer can only vaguely trace, and in a way which would be subject to the instability of all hypotheses, which are varied and complicated by an infinity of circumstances too difficult to foresee and to combine."

One would think it was a professor of agriculture who was saying to his pupils--"The climate is the only rule for the agriculturist. Hisresources dictate to him his duties. The first thing he has to consider is his local position. If he is on a clayey soil, he must do so and so. If he has to contend with sand, this is the way in which he must set about it. Every facility is open to the agriculturist who wishes to clear and improve his soil. If he only has the skill, the manure which he has at his disposal will suggest to him a plan of operation, which a professor can only vaguely trace, and in a way that would be subject to the uncertainty of all hypotheses, which vary and are complicated by an infinity of circumstances too difficult to foresee and to combine."

But, oh! sublime writers, deign to remember sometimes that this clay, this sand, this manure, of which you are disposing in so arbitrary a manner, are men, your equals, intelligent and free beings like yourselves, who have received from God, as you have, the faculty of seeing, of foreseeing, of thinking, and of judging for themselves!

Mably. (He is supposing the laws to be worn out by time and by the neglect of security, and continues thus):--

"Under these circumstances, we must be convinced that the springs of Government are relaxed. Give them a new tension (it is the reader who is addressed), and the evil will be remedied.... Think lees of punishing the faults than of encouraging the virtues which you want. By this method you will bestow upon your republic the vigour of youth. Through ignorance of this, a free people has lost its liberty! But if the evil has made so much way that the ordinary magistrates are unable to remedy it effectually, have recourse to an extraordinary magistracy, whose time should be short, and its power considerable. The imagination of the citizens requires to be impressed."

In this style he goes on through twenty volumes.

There was a time when, under the influence of teaching like this, which is the root of classical education, every one was for placing himself beyond and above mankind, for the sake of arranging, organising, and instituting it in his own way.

Condillac.--"Take upon yourself, my lord, the character of Lycurgus or of Solon. Before you finish reading this essay, amuse yourself with giving laws to some wild people in America or in Africa. Establish these roving men in fixed dwellings; teach them to keep flocks.... Endeavour to develop the social qualities which nature has implanted in them.... Make them begin to practise the duties of humanity.... Cause the pleasures of the passions to become distasteful to them by punishments, and you will see these barbarians, with every plan of your legislation, lose a vice and gain a virtue.

"All these people have had laws. But few among them have been happy. Why is this? Because legislators have almost always been ignorant of the object of society, which is, to unite families by a common interest.

"Impartiality in law consists in two things:--in establishing equality in the fortunes and in the dignity of the citizens.... In proportion to the degree of equality established by the laws, the dearer will they become to every citizen.... How can avarice, ambition, dissipation, idleness, sloth, envy, hatred, or jealousy, agitate men who are equal in fortune and dignity, and to whom the laws leave no hope of disturbing their equality?

"What has been told you of the republic of Sparta ought to enlighten you on this question. No other State has had laws more in accordance with the order of nature or of equality."

It is not to be wondered at that the 17th and 18th centuries should have looked upon the human race as inert matter, ready to receive everything, form, figure, impulse, movement, and life, from a great prince, or a great legislator, or a great genius. These ages were reared in the study of antiquity, and antiquity presents everywhere, in Egypt, Persia, Greece, and Rome, the spectacle of a few men moulding mankind according to their fancy, and mankind to this end enslaved by force or by imposture. And what does this prove? That because men and society are improvable, error, ignorance, despotism, slavery, and superstition must be more prevalent in early times. The mistake of the writers quoted above, is not that they have asserted this fact, but that they have proposed it, as a rule, for the admiration and imitation of future generations. Their mistake has been, with an inconceivable absence of discernment, and upon the faith of a puerile conventionalism, that they have admitted what is inadmissible, viz., the grandeur, dignity, morality, and well-being of the artificial societies of the ancient world; they have not understood that time produces and spreads enlightenment; and that in proportion to the increase of enlightenment, right ceases to be upheld by force, and society regains possession of herself.

And, in fact, what is the political work which we are endeavouring to promote? It is no other than the instinctive effort of every people towards liberty. And what is liberty, whose name can make every heart beat, and which can agitate the world, but the union of all liberties, the liberty of conscience, of instruction, of association, of the press, of locomotion, of labour, and of exchange; in other words, the free exercise, for all, of all the inoffensive faculties; and again, in other words, the destruction of all despotisms, even of legal despotism, and the reduction of law to its only rational sphere, which is to regulate the individual right of legitimate defence, or to repress injustice?

This tendency of the human race, it must be admitted, is greatly thwarted, particularly in our country, by the fatal disposition, resulting from classical teaching, and common to all politicians, of placing themselves beyond mankind, to arrange, organise, and regulate it, according to their fancy.

For whilst society is struggling to realise liberty, the great men who place themselves at its head, imbued with the principles of the seventeenth and eighteenth centuries, think only of subjecting it to the philanthropic despotism of their social inventions, and making it bear with docility, according to the expression of Rousseau, the yoke of public felicity, as pictured in their own imaginations.

This was particularly the case in 1789. No sooner was the old system destroyed, than society was to be submitted to other artificial arrangements, always with the same starting-point--the omnipotence of the law.

Saint Just.--"The legislator commands the future. It is for him to will for the good of mankind. It is for him to make men what he wishes them to be."

Robespierre.--"The function of Government is to direct the physical and moral powers of the nation towards the object of its institution."

Billaud Varennes.--"A people who are to be restored to liberty must be formed anew. Ancient prejudices must be destroyed, antiquated customs changed, depraved affections corrected, inveterate vices eradicated. For this, a strong force and a vehement impulse will be necessary.... Citizens, the inflexible austerity of Lycurgus created the firm basis of the Spartan republic. The feeble and trusting disposition of Solon plunged Athens into slavery. This parallel contains the whole science of Government."

Lepelletier.--"Considering the extent of human degradation, I am convinced of the necessity of effecting an entire regeneration of the race, and, if I may so express myself, of creating a new people."

Men, therefore, are nothing but raw material. It is not for them to will their own improvement. They are not capable of it; according to Saint Just, it is only the legislator who is. Men are merely to be what he wills that they should be. According to Robespierre, who copies Rousseau literally, the legislator is to begin by assigning the aim of the institutions of the nation. After this, the Government has only to direct all its physical and moral forces towards this end. All this time the nation itself is to remain perfectly passive; and Billaud Varennes would teach us that it ought to have no prejudices, affections, nor wants, but such as are authorised by the legislator. He even goes so far as to say that the inflexible austerity of a man is the basis of a republic.

We have seen that, in cases where the evil is so great that the ordinary magistrates are unable to remedy it, Mably recommends a dictatorship, to promote virtue. "Have recourse," says he, "to an extraordinary magistracy, whose time shall be short, and his power considerable. The imagination of the people requires to be impressed." This doctrine has not been neglected. Listen to Robespierre:--

"The principle of the Republican Government is virtue, and the means to be adopted, during its establishment, is terror. We want to substitute, in our country, morality for egotism, probity for honour, principles for customs, duties for decorum, the empire of reason for the tyranny of fashion, contempt of vice for contempt of misfortune, pride for insolence, greatness of soul for vanity, love of glory for love of money, good people for good company, merit for intrigue, genius for wit, truth for glitter, the charm of happiness for the weariness of pleasure, the greatness of man for the littleness of the great, a magnanimous, powerful, happy people, for one that is easy, frivolous, degraded; that is to say, we would substitute all the virtues and miracles of a republic for all the vices and absurdities of monarchy."

At what a vast height above the rest of mankind does Robespierre place himself here! And observe the arrogance with which he speaks. He is not content with expressing a desire for a great renovation of the human heart, he does not even expect such a result from a regular Government. No; he intends to effect it himself, and by means of terror. The object of the discourse from which this puerile and laborious mass of antithesis is extracted, was to exhibit the principles of morality which ought to direct a revolutionary Government. Moreover, when Robespierre asks for a dictatorship, it is not merely for the purpose of repelling a foreign enemy, or of putting down factions; it is that he may establish, by means of terror, and as a preliminary to the game of the Constitution, his own principles of morality. He pretends to nothing short of extirpating from the country, by means of terror, egotism, honour, customs, decorum, fashion, vanity, the love of money, good company, intrigue, wit, luxury, and misery. It is not until after he, Robespierre, shall have accomplished these miracles, as he rightly calls them, that he will allow the law to regain her empire. Truly, it would be well if these visionaries, who think so much of themselves and so little of mankind, who want to renew everything, would only be content with trying to reform themselves, the task would be arduous enough for them. In general, however, these gentlemen, the reformers, legislators, and politicians, do not desire to exercise an immediate despotism over mankind. No, they are too moderate and too philanthropic for that. They only contend for the despotism, the absolutism, the omnipotence of the law. They aspire only to make the law.

To show how universal this strange disposition has been in France, I had need not only to have copied the whole of the works of Mably, Raynal, Rousseau, Fenelon, and to have made long extracts from Bossuet and Montesquieu, but to have given the entire transactions of the sittings of the Convention, I shall do no such thing, however, but merely refer the reader to them.

It is not to be wondered at that this idea should have suited Buonaparte exceedingly well. He embraced it with ardour, and put it in practice with energy. Playing the part of a chemist, Europe was to him the material for his experiments. But this material reacted against him. More than half undeceived, Buonaparte, at St. Helena, seemed to admit that there is an initiative in every people, and he became less hostile to liberty. Yet this did not prevent him from giving this lesson to his son in his will:--"To govern, is to diffuse morality, education, and well-being."

After all this, I hardly need show, by fastidious quotations, the opinions of Morelly, Babeuf, Owen, Saint Simon, and Fourier. I shall confine myself to a few extracts from Louis Blanc's book on the organisation of labour.

"In our project, society receives the impulse of power." (Page 126.)

In what does the impulse which power gives to society consist? In imposing upon it the project of M. Louis Blanc.

On the other hand, society is the human race. The human race, then, is to receive its impulse from M. Louis Blanc.

It is at liberty to do so or not, it will be said. Of course the human race is at liberty to take advice from anybody, whoever it may be. But this is not the way in which M. Louis Blanc understands the thing. He means that his project should be converted into law, and, consequently, forcibly imposed by power.

"In our project, the State has only to give a legislation to labour, by means of which the industrial movement may and ought to be accomplished in all liberty. It (the State) merely places society on an incline (that is all) that it may descend, when once it is placed there, by the mere force of things, and by the natural course of the established mechanism."

But what is this incline? One indicated by M. Louis Blanc. Does it not lead to an abyss? No, it leads to happiness. Why, then, does not society go there of itself? Because it does not know what it wants, and it requires an impulse. What is to give it this impulse? Power. And who is to give the impulse to power? The inventor of the machine, M. Louis Blanc.

We shall never get out of this circle--mankind passive, and a great man moving it by the intervention of the law.

Once on this incline, will society enjoy something like liberty? Without a doubt. And what is liberty?

"Once for all: liberty consists, not only in the right granted, but in the power given to man, to exercise, to develop his faculties under the empire of justice, and under the protection of the law.

"And this is no vain distinction; there is a deep meaning in it, and its consequences are not to be estimated. For when once it is admitted that man, to be truly free, must have the power to exercise and develop his faculties, it follows that every member of society has a claim upon it for such instruction as shall enable it to display itself, and for the instruments of labour, without which human activity can find no scope. Now, by whose intervention is society to give to each of its members the requisite instruction and the necessary instruments of labour, unless by that of the State?"

Thus, liberty is power. In what does this power consist? In possessing instruction and instruments of labour. Who is to give instruction and instruments of labour? Society, who owes them. By whose intervention is society to give instruments of labour to those who do not possess them?

By the intervention of the State. From whom is the State to obtain them?

It is for the reader to answer this question, and to notice whither all this tends.

One of the strangest phenomena of our time, and one which will probably be a matter of astonishment to our descendants, is the doctrine which is founded upon this triple hypothesis: the radical passiveness of mankind,--the omnipotence of the law,--the infallibility of the legislator:--this is the sacred symbol of the party which proclaims itself exclusively democratic.

It is true that it professes also to be social.

So far as it is democratic, it, has an unlimited faith in mankind.

So far as it is social, it places it beneath the mud.

Are political rights under discussion? Is a legislator to be chosen? Oh! then the people possess science by instinct: they are gifted with an admirable tact; their will is always right; the general will cannot err. Suffrage cannot be too universal. Nobody is under any responsibility to society. The will and the capacity to choose well are taken for granted. Can the people be mistaken? Are we not living in an age of enlightenment? What! are the people to be always kept in leading strings? Have they not acquired their rights at the cost of effort and sacrifice? Have they not given sufficient proof of intelligence and wisdom? Are they not arrived at maturity? Are they not in a state to judge for themselves? Do they not know their own interest? Is there a man or a class who would dare to claim the right of putting himself in the place of the people, of deciding and of acting for them? No, no; the people would be free, and they shall be so. They wish to conduct their own affairs, and they shall do so.

But when once the legislator is duly elected, then indeed the style of his speech alters. The nation is sent back into passiveness, inertness, nothingness, and the legislator takes possession of omnipotence. It is for him to invent, for him to direct, for him to impel, for him to organise. Mankind has nothing to do but to submit; the hour of despotism has struck. And we must observe that this is decisive; for the people, just before so enlightened, so moral, so perfect, have no inclinations at all, or, if they have any, they all lead them downwards towards degradation. And yet they ought to have a little liberty! But are we not assured, by M. Considerant, that liberty leads fatally to monopoly? Are we not told that liberty is competition? and that competition, according to M. Louis Blanc,is a system of extermination for the people, and of ruination for trade? For that reason people are exterminated and ruined in proportion as they are free--take, for example, Switzerland, Holland, England, and the United States? Does not M. Louis Blanc tell us again, that competition leads to monopoly, and that, for the same reason, cheapness leads to exorbitant prices? That competition tends to drain the sources of consumption, and urges production to a destructive activity? That competition forces production to increase, and consumption to decrease;--whence it follows that free people produce for the sake of not consuming; that there is nothing but oppression and madness among them; and that it is absolutely necessary for M. Louis Blanc to see to it?

What sort of liberty should be allowed to men? Liberty of conscience?--But we should see them all profiting by the permission to become atheists. Liberty of education?--But parents would be paying professors to teach their sons immorality and error; besides, if we are to believe M. Thiers, education, if left to the national liberty, would cease to be national, and we should be educating our children in the ideas of the Turks or Hindoos, instead of which, thanks to the legal despotism of the universities, they have the good fortune to be educated in the noble ideas of the Romans. Liberty of labour?--But this is only competition, whose effect is to leave all productions unconsumed, to exterminate the people, and to ruin the tradesmen. The liberty of exchange?--But it is well known that the protectionists have shown, over and over again, that a man must be ruined when he exchanges freely, and that to become rich it is necessary to exchange without liberty. Liberty of association?--But, according to the socialist doctrine, liberty and association exclude each other, for the liberty of men is attacked just to force them to associate.

You must see, then, that the socialist democrats cannot in conscience allow men any liberty, because, by their own nature, they tend in every instance to all kinds of degradation and demoralisation.

We are therefore left to conjecture, in this case, upon what foundation universal suffrage is claimed for them with so much importunity.

The pretensions of organisers suggest another question, which I have often asked them, and to which I am not aware that I ever received an answer:-- Since the natural tendencies of mankind are so bad that it is not safe to allow them liberty, how comes it to pass that the tendencies of organisers are always good? Do not the legislators and their agents form a part of the human race? Do they consider that they are composed of different materials from the rest of mankind? They say that society, when left to itself, rushes to inevitable destruction, because its instincts are perverse. They pretend, to stop it in its downward course, and to give it a better direction. They have, therefore, received from heaven, intelligence and virtues which place them beyond and above mankind: let them show their title to this superiority. They would be our shepherds, and we are to be their flock. This arrangement presupposes in them a natural superiority, the right to which we are fully justified in calling upon them to prove.

You must observe that I am not contending against their right to invent social combinations, to propagate them, to recommend them, and to try them upon themselves, at their own expense and risk; but I do dispute their right to impose them upon us through the medium of the law, that is, by force and by public taxes.

I would not insist upon the Cabetists, the Fourierists, the Proudhonians, the Universitaries, and the Protectionists renouncing their own particular ideas; I would only have them renounce that idea which is common to them all,--viz., that of subjecting us by force to their own groups and series to their social workshops, to their gratuitous bank to their Græco-Romano morality, and to their commercial restrictions. I would ask them to allow us the faculty of judging of their plans, and not to oblige us to adopt them, if we find that they hurt our interests or are repugnant to our consciences.

To presume to have recourse to power and taxation, besides being oppressive and unjust, implies further, the injurious supposition that the organiser is infallible, and mankind incompetent.

And if mankind is not competent to judge for itself, why do they talk so much about universal suffrage?

This contradiction in ideas is unhappily to be found also in facts; and whilst the French nation has preceded all others in obtaining its rights, or rather its political claims, this has by no means prevented it from being more governed, and directed, and imposed upon, and fettered, and cheated, than any other nation. It is also the one, of all others, where revolutions are constantly to be dreaded, and it is perfectly natural that it should be so.

So long as this idea is retained, which is admitted by all our politicians, and so energetically expressed by M. Louis Blanc in these words--"Society receives its impulse from power;" so long as men consider themselves as capable of feeling, yet passive--incapable of raising themselves by their own discernment and by their own energy to any morality, or well-being, and while they expect everything from the law; in a word, while they admit that their relations with the State are the same as those of the flock with the shepherd, it is clear that the responsibility of power is immense. Fortune and misfortune, wealth and destitution, equality and inequality, all proceed from it. It is charged with everything, it undertakes everything, it does everything; therefore it has to answer for everything. If we are happy, it has a right to claim our gratitude; but if we are miserable, it alone must bear the blame. Are not our persons and property, in fact, at its disposal? Is not the law omnipotent? In creating the universitary monopoly, it has engaged to answer the expectations of fathers of families who have been deprived of liberty; and if these expectations are disappointed, whose fault is it? In regulating industry, it has engaged to make it prosper, otherwise it would have been absurd to deprive it of its liberty; and if it suffers, whose fault is it? In pretending to adjust the balance of commerce by the game of tariffs, it engages to make it prosper; and if, so far from prospering, it is destroyed, whose fault is it? In granting its protection to maritime armaments in exchange for their liberty, it has engaged to render them lucrative; if they become burdensome, whose fault is it?

Thus, there is not a grievance in the nation for which the Government does not voluntarily make itself responsible. Is it to be wondered at that every failure threatens to cause a revolution?

And what is the remedy proposed? To extend indefinitely the dominion of the law, i.e., the responsibility of Government. But if the Government engages to raise and to regulate wages, and is not able to do it; if it engages to assist all those who are in want, and is not able to do it; if it engages to provide an asylum for every labourer, and is not able to do it; if it engages to offer to all such as are eager to borrow, gratuitous credit, and is not able to do it; if, in words which we regret should have escaped the pen of M. de Lamartine, "the State considers that its mission is to enlighten, to develop, to enlarge, to strengthen, to spiritualize, and to sanctify the soul of the people,"--if it fails in this, is it not evident that after every disappointment, which, alas! is more than probable, there will be a no less inevitable revolution?

I shall now resume the subject by remarking, that immediately after the economical part10 of the question, and at the entrance of the political part, a leading question presents itself? It is the following:--

What is law? What ought it to be? What is its domain? What are its limits? Where, in fact, does the prerogative of the legislator stop?

I have no hesitation in answering, Law is common force organised to prevent injustice;--in short, Law is Justice.

It is not true that the legislator has absolute power over our persons and property, since they pre-exist, and his work is only to secure them from injury.

It is not true that the mission of the law is to regulate our consciences, our ideas, our will, our education, our sentiments, our works, our exchanges, our gifts, our enjoyments. Its mission is to prevent the rights of one from interfering with those of another, in any one of these things.

Law, because it has force for its necessary sanction, can only have as its lawful domain the domain of force, which is justice.

And as every individual has a right to have recourse to force only in cases of lawful defence, so collective force, which is only the union of individual forces, cannot be rationally used for any other end.

The law, then, is solely the organisation of individual rights, which existed before legitimate defence.

Law is justice.

So far from being able to oppress the persons of the people, or to plunder their property, even for a philanthropic end, its mission is to protect the former, and to secure to them the possession of the latter.

It must not be said, either, that it may be philanthropic, so long as it abstains from all oppression; for this is a contradiction. The law cannot avoid acting upon our persons and property; if it does not secure them, it violates them if it touches them.

The law is justice.

Nothing can be more clear and simple, more perfectly defined and bounded, or more visible to every eye; for justice is a given quantity, immutable and unchangeable, and which admits of neither increase or diminution.

Depart from this point, make the law religious, fraternal, equalising, industrial, literary, or artistic, and you will be lost in vagueness and uncertainty; you will be upon unknown ground, in a forced Utopia, or, which is worse, in the midst of a multitude of Utopias, striving to gain possession of the law, and to impose it upon you; for fraternity and philanthropy have no fixed limits, like justice. Where will you stop? Where is the law to stop? One person, as M. de Saint Cricq, will only extend his philanthropy to some of the industrial classes, and will require the law to dispose of the consumers in favour of the producers. Another, like M. Considerant, will take up the cause of the working classes, and claim for them by means of the law, at a fixed rate, clothing, lodging, food, and everything necessary for the support of life. A third, as, M. Louis Blanc, will say, and with reason, that this would be an incomplete fraternity, and that the law ought to provide them with instruments of labour and the means of instruction. A fourth will observe that such an arrangement still leaves room for inequality, and that the law ought to introduce into the most remote hamlets luxury, literature, and the arts. This is the high road to communism; in other words, legislation will be--what it now is--the battle-field for everybody's dreams and everybody's covetousness.

Law is justice.

In this proposition we represent to ourselves a simple, immovable Government. And I defy any one to tell me whence the thought of a revolution, an insurrection, or a simple disturbance could arise against a public force confined to the repression of injustice. Under such a system, there would be more well-being, and this well-being would be more equally distributed; and as to the sufferings inseparable from humanity, no one would think of accusing the Government of them, for it would be as innocent of them as it is of the variations of the temperature. Have the people ever been known to rise against the court of repeals, or assail the justices of the peace, for the sake of claiming the rate of wages, gratuitous credit, instruments of labour, the advantages of the tariff, or the social workshop? They know perfectly well that these combinations are beyond the jurisdiction of the justices of the peace, and they would soon learn that they are not within the jurisdiction of the law.

But if the law were to be made upon the principle of fraternity, if it were to be proclaimed that from it proceed all benefits and all evils--that it is responsible for every individual grievance and for every social inequality--then you open the door to an endless succession of complaints, irritations, troubles, and revolutions.

Law is justice.

And it would be very strange if it could properly be anything else! Is not justice right? Are not rights equal? With what show of right can the law interfere to subject me to the social plans of MM. Mimerel, de Melun, Thiers, or Louis Blanc, rather than to subject these gentlemen to my plans? Is it to be supposed that Nature has not bestowed upon ME sufficient imagination to invent a Utopia too? Is it for the law to make choice of one amongst so many fancies, and to make use of the public force in its service?

Law is justice.

And let it not be said, as it continually is, that the law, in this sense, would be atheistic, individual, and heartless, and that it would make mankind wear its own image. This is an absurd conclusion, quite worthy of the governmental infatuation which sees mankind in the law.

What then? Does it follow that, if we are free, we shall cease to act? Does it follow, that if we do not receive an impulse from the law, we shall receive no impulse at all? Does it follow, that if the law confines itself to securing to us the free exercise of our faculties, our faculties will be paralyzed? Does it follow, that if the law does not impose upon us forms of religion, modes of association, methods of instruction, rules for labour, directions for exchange, and plans for charity, we shall plunge eagerly into atheism, isolation, ignorance, misery, and egotism? Does it follow, that we shall no longer recognise the power and goodness of God; that we shall cease to associate together, to help each other, to love and assist our unfortunate brethren, to study the secrets of nature, and to aspire after perfection in our existence?

Law is justice.

And it is under the law of justice, under the reign of right, under the influence of liberty, security, stability, and responsibility, that every man will attain to the measure of his worth, to all the dignity of his being, and that mankind will accomplish, with order and with calmness--slowly, it is true, but with certainty--the progress decreed to it.

I believe that my theory is correct; for whatever be the question upon which I am arguing, whether it be religious, philosophical, political, or economical; whether it affects well-being, morality, equality, right, justice, progress, responsibility, property, labour, exchange, capital, wages, taxes, population, credit, or Government; at whatever point of the scientific horizon I start from, I invariably come to the same thing--the solution of the social problem is in liberty.

And have I not experience on my side? Cast your eye over the globe. Which are the happiest, the most moral, and the most peaceable nations? Those where the law interferes the least with private activity; where the Government is the least felt; where individuality has the most scope, and public opinion the most influence; where the machinery of the administration is the least important and the least complicated; where taxation is lightest and least unequal, popular discontent the least excited and the least justifiable; where the responsibility of individuals and classes is the most active, and where, consequently, if morals are not in a perfect state, at any rate they tend incessantly to correct themselves; where transactions, meetings, and associations are the least fettered; where labour, capital, and production suffer the least from artificial displacements; where mankind follows most completely its own natural course; where the thought of God prevails the most over the inventions of men; those, in short, who realise the most nearly this idea--That within the limits of right, all should flow from the free, perfectible, and voluntary action of man; nothing be attempted by the law or by force, except the administration of universal justice.

I cannot avoid coming to this conclusion--that there are too many great men in the world; there are too many legislators, organisers, institutors of society, conductors of the people, fathers of nations, &c., &c. Too many persons place themselves above mankind, to rule and patronize it; too many persons make a trade of attending to it. It will be answered:--"You yourself are occupied upon it all this time." Very true. But it must be admitted that it is in another sense entirely that I am speaking; and if I join the reformers it is solely for the purpose of inducing them to relax their hold.

I am not doing as Vaucauson did with his automaton, but as a physiologist does with the organisation of the human frame; I would study and admire it.

I am acting with regard to it in the spirit which animated a celebrated traveller. He found himself in the midst of a savage tribe. A child had just been born, and a crowd of soothsayers, magicians, and quacks were around it, armed with rings, hooks, and bandages. One said--"This child will never smell the perfume of a calumet, unless I stretch his nostrils." Another said--"He will be without the sense of hearing, unless I draw his ears down to his shoulders." A third said--"He will never see the light of the sun, unless I give his eyes an oblique direction." A fourth said--"He will never be upright, unless I bend his legs." A fifth said--"He will not be able to think, unless I press his brain." "Stop!" said the traveller. "Whatever God does, is well done; do not pretend to know more than He; and as He has given organs to this frail creature, allow those organs to develop themselves, to strengthen themselves by exercise, use, experience, and liberty."

God has implanted in mankind, also, all that is necessary to enable it to accomplish its destinies. There is a providential social physiology, as well as a providential human physiology. The social organs are constituted so as to enable them to develop harmoniously in the grand air of liberty. Away, then, with quacks and organisers! Away with their rings, and their chains, and their hooks, and their pincers! Away with their artificial methods! Away with their social workshops, their governmental whims, their centralization, their tariffs, their universities, their State religions, their gratuitous or monopolising banks, their limitations, their restrictions, their moralisations, and their equalisation by taxation! And now, after having vainly inflicted upon the social body so many systems, let them end where they ought to have begun--reject all systems, and make trial of liberty--of liberty, which is an act of faith in God and in His work.